teen chat

teen chat

Online Conversations
About Important Stuff

Mike Yorkey

VINE
BOOKS

SERVANT PUBLICATIONS
ANN ARBOR, MICHIGAN

Vine Books is an imprint of Servant Publications especially designed to serve evangelical Christians.

"Charting a Different Course" by Mike Yorkey, *Focus on the Family* magazine, November 1992, Vol. 16, No. 11, published by Focus on the Family. © 1992. All rights reserved. International copyright secured. Used by permission.

Published by Servant Publications
P.O. Box 8617
Ann Arbor, Michigan 48107

Cover design: DesignTeam, Grand Rapids, MI

00 01 02 10 9 8 7 6 5 4

Printed in the United States of America
ISBN 1-56955-076-X

LIBRARY OF CONGRESS CATALOGING-IN-PUBLICATION DATA

Teen chat : on-line conversations about important stuff / [edited by] Mike Yorkey.
    p.   cm.
  ISBN 1-56955-076-X (alk. paper)
    1. Teenagers—Religious life—Miscellanea.   2. Christian life—Miscellanea.
I. Yorkey, Mike.
BV4531.2.T44 1999
248.8'3—dc21
                                     99-12821
                                     CIP

Dedication

To Richard and Dee Dee Stephens
for the countless lives you've changed for Christ

Contents

Introduction

Have you ever logged on to America Online or the Internet and found yourself in a "chat room"? If so, then you've probably watched the "chat" unfold on your computer screen, and perhaps you've even jumped into cyberspace and typed messages to others. At any rate, scrolling through the dialogue was probably pretty fun.

Well, we're taking the same approach to this book. Pretend that you've turned on your computer, did a Yahoo search for "Teen Advisors Chat Room," and found yourself here. What you're about to read is some great advice and interesting stories from the Teen Advisors* in a chat room format. These TAs are real people, but I've changed their names to protect their identities since they are not adults. But six people who've been with Teen Advisors a long time and are now in their early twenties appear in the book with their real names. They are: Jennifer Young (TA.Jen), Missy Newlin (TA.Missy), Anne Partin (TA.Anne), Mary Lawson Stephens (TA.ML), and Mike Holt (TA.Mike).

Got how it works? Good. Turn the page and log on!

—Mike Yorkey, your TA.Host

---

* Throughout the book you'll hear about Teen Advisors. Teen Advisors (TAs) is a peer support ministry to teens. The purpose of the group is to help teens live for Christ and not give in to negative peer pressure all around them. Teens who join TA sign a contract that states they will not drink, smoke, do drugs, or engage in other kinds of behavior that are harmful to them and are inconsistent with Christian morals. You'll read more about TAs later in this book.

A Word About Chat Rooms

Chat rooms can be a fun way to "talk" with people on the computer, to exchange ideas, and even to share your faith. On the other hand, chat rooms can also be huge waste of time—or even a source of temptation or danger—if you aren't careful. Here are some important principles for you to keep in mind if you ever check out a real chat room.

Be Safe. Be Smart. Before you go online, talk with your parents beforehand about how much time you can spend on the computer, and what "chat rooms" are safe for you to use. Many service providers offer chat rooms keyed to particular interest, including chat rooms for Christian teens.

You can find Christian web sites and chat rooms by searching the Internet under "Christian chat rooms" or "Christian teens." Have a parent sit with you at first to check out the possible sites, and decide together which ones are OK for you to visit.

Protect yourself—and your family. Some people use the Internet to exploit those they encounter online, financially or otherwise. So it's not a good idea to give out personal information such as your real name, address, or phone numbers, unless your parents give you permission. Never give your computer passwords for *any* reason.

Remember, people in chat rooms are not always who they claim to be. If you decide you'd like to meet a "chat room friend," always check with your parents first (they may want to come with you for your own safety), and meet in a public place. For your own safety, protect your privacy. This is not being paranoid—this is being SMART!

Remember to glorify God even when you're online. Before you go online, ask the Lord to help you honor your parents' guidelines, and to protect you from seeing things you shouldn't. If at any time the conversation online becomes too personal or includes language or topics that make you uncomfortable, log off—and notify the chat room administrator (who has the power to kick people out of the chat room if they get rude or crude!). The psalmist said it best:

> I will walk in my house with blameless heart.
> I will set before my eyes no vile thing.
>
> **PSALM 101:2B-3 NIV**

A Guide to "Teen Chat"

If you've ever been in a chat room before, you may have noticed that people use lots of little abbreviations and symbols to add meaning to the words they type. Here is a short list of commonly used keystrokes and their meanings:

: O]   :-]~   :-]   >8-]

Happy Faces
(used when someone is smiling or teasing)

:O[:-{   :^[

Sad Faces
(used when someone is disappointed or mad)

;O]

Wink
(used when someone is joking)

>8-0   =8>0   :-0

Gaping Mouth
(used when someone is confused or surprised)

LOL = Lots of Laughs
IMHO = In My Humble Opinion
TTFN = "Ta-ta for Now" (signing off)

one

Let's Chat: How Do You Feel About You Today?

TA.Host:	*What would you say is the biggest "hot button" for teens today?*
MeghanM:	Self-esteem and how we feel about ourselves.
Tom0483:	Self-esteem? Not me. I'm #1! LOL
SheriBabe:	Meghan's right. It's hard to feel good about yourself when you've got family problems, school pressure, relationships problems, not to mention everyday pressures of fitting in.
BANDIT16:	I know someone who throws up everything she eats, just to keep her weight down so she looks good. It's gross, but she does it anyway.
Tom0483:	Yuck! >8-0
SheriBabe:	Lots of kids battle eating disorders. It's hard to know what to say to a friend when you know she's in trouble like that.
MeghanM	Do you know about Teen Advisors? I'm really thankful for them. A huge part of what Teen Advisors does is to allow us teens, maybe for the first time in our lives, to really talk to each other. By talking to each other we realize that we're not the only ones with problems.

Jimmy.S-15:	How do TAs talk to each other?
MeghanM:	It's hard at first. It means letting down your guard and not pretending to be cool all the time. It means letting other people into your life in a big way. TA is a good way for some of the shy kids—the ones on the fringes, the loners—to make some friends. I've been a shy kid.
Allie98:	Me too. Talking online is easier. Cuz you don't have to worry about what you're wearing, or how you look. I hate it when people make fun of me!
MeghanM:	I know how you feel, Allie. :0) Everybody feels that way sometimes. That's why TA is great. At our retreats and meetings and online we talk about how to build up our self-esteem. It helps to talk about how to handle the pressures at school and everywhere else. How to be ourselves when everyone around us tells us what to look like and be like—what clothes we wear, and what's cool.
Tom0483:	Who cares? Gotta be ME! Unless some girl thinks I'm a dork, of course. Speaking of which, my girlfriend's on the other line. Bye!
BANDIT16:	Yeah—or parents hassle you about your haircut. :-(
TA.Host:	*How does Teen Advisors help you cope with what everyone (the world) is telling you to do?*
MeghanM:	TA gives us a totally different perspective. At retreats and stuff we learn what the Bible says about us ... that we are a new creation. Then we can replace the world's lies with God's

	truth. That's where true self-confidence comes from.
SheriBabe:	Whoa! The BIBLE? Talks about US? No way!
Allie98:	What kind of stuff does it say? I thought it was just full of stories like Jonah and the whale …
MeghanM:	Well, for example, I once heard a speaker say that circumstances sometimes dictate a person's self-esteem, whether they're born into a family of abuse, divorce, or get an eating disorder. But when you know Jesus Christ, you're not limited by circumstances. Our past doesn't have to dictate how we view ourselves. Changing our self-view is not an overnight process, but it's lifelong and takes place every day.
SheriBabe:	My mom says no one can really know if God exists. Anyway, I have to go. TTFN.
BANDIT16:	I believe God exists. But I don't know if you can know God personally. I mean, who wants God watching you every minute?!
Leslie4U:	I know what you mean. I am one of those people who is unusually good at hiding how I'm really feeling. Even my close friends never know what's going on inside of me.
Tbubbles:	Hello, everybody. Leslie, I have a friend who is just like you, who always hides what she is feeling. Why do you do that?
Leslie4U:	Because I don't know how to explain what I'm feeling. So it's easier to hide my feelings by smiling, laughing, and acting like I am having the time of my life. When I'm feeling sad and depressed, I just climb into my little shell.
Tbubbles:	You sound really down. Is it really that bad? :-(

Leslie4U:	Sometimes. I know I have many things going for me. I am a cheerleader, I make good grades, I have loving parents who would do anything for me, and I have a relationship with God. But I still don't feel good about myself, and so those things haven't helped at all. I envy people for how they look or what they wear, then I hear them complain about their lives and it makes me even more sad and depressed.
BANDIT16:	Boy, now you're getting me down.
Leslie4U:	I have been told that I am a pessimistic person, and that many times, instead of finding the good in something, I only find the bad. But I can tell you what has helped me.
BANDIT16:	What???????????
Leslie4U:	It's little things, really. A simple smile or a warm hello from a good friend can brighten my whole day. If I know someone cares about me and is there for me, I feel more secure. People who are depressed or sad don't always change instantly. But it means a lot to know someone cares.:0) I hear my mom calling—gotta go. TTFN.
Allie98:	Leslie's right. Having a real friend can really help you through tough times. But it's hard to reach out when you're hurting. If you mope around and sit in the corner, a lot of your friends will not want to be around you too much. It's a tough balance: if you wallow in self-pity, no one wants to be with you. But if you fake it, people know.

MeghanM: That's why knowing God is so great. He knows exactly how you feel and loves you anyway. Even when you don't like yourself very much!

TA.Host: *Thanks for sharing about fighting bad self-esteem. Tell me, what are some things that Teen Advisors is doing to teach teens to feel better about themselves?*

TA.Mike: Teen Advisors help you understand how God created you and your personality. TAs learn that it's OK to be yourself and that there are going to be many times when you are going to feel worthless and unloved. The thing to remember is that we all have worth before God, who loves us no matter what. The more we appreciate who we are and what God created us to be, the more comfortable we will be with our self-image.

TA.Host: *What kind of problems did you have with self-esteem?*

TA.Mike: Early on I caught on to what a popular person was supposed to be like in junior high, and trained myself to act that way around certain people. But because I was mimicking other people, I wasn't being myself. And no matter how hard I tried, I would say dumb things in front of the crowd. I sure felt worthless. I always ate lunch by myself. I was scared. I didn't like myself.

TA.ML:	I know what you mean. When I went to a private high school, I had to take an entrance exam, a test that decides which "track" you'll be placed in: remedial, basic, or accelerated. Well, I didn't test too well, which means I was put in the remedial track. At first I tried to laugh it off—but it really got to me. I stopped trying in my schoolwork. Since I didn't feel smart, I figured, why bother? I never did my homework. I never studied for a test.
TA.Host:	*Then what happened?*
TA.ML:	My sophomore year, maybe my junior year, the principal called me into his office and told me that he saw a lot of leadership potential in me. He said I needed to step up and take an active role on campus. That next school year, I became captain of the cheerleading squad and an officer in the VIP club. Today, I'm really glad that principal pulled me aside and said that I had something important to contribute. As simple as that sounds, his few words of encouragement helped me to begin seeing myself differently.
TA.Host:	*Sometimes a simple word or two of encouragement can make a big difference. Are there others online who have wrestled with the issue of self-esteem?*
Ashley99:	I think it's impossible to go through adolescence without any self-esteem problems. I had a really carefree childhood, but then in third

	grade, I had acquired a nickname that I despise to this day. My friends started calling me "Miss Perfect."
BANDIT16:	LOL Kids at school used to call me "Gimp" cuz I was always hurting myself. Hey … gotta get to soccer practice. Bye, all.
Tbubbles:	How about "Space Girl"? :0(
Allie98:	It's better than no one talking to you at all …
Ashley99:	I don't know about that. I was always good in school, and loved to answer all the teacher's questions. I think my friends and classmates resented this, which is why they started calling me "Miss Perfect." Pretty soon I started worrying about whether I was talking too much, answering too many questions, or looking too interested. I learned back in the third grade that such actions weren't cool.
ChillyBilly:	So you were a real goody-goody, huh? There was one kid in my class like that … he used to get stuffed in a locker at least once a week!
Ashley99:	Yeah, well no one put me in a locker, but it still was no fun. So when I went to high school, I decided I needed a new image. No more "Miss Perfect."
TA.ML:	What did you do?
Ashley99:	Everything I could think of to fit in with other students around me. I traded my clean-cut outfits for the grunge look, and I bought an $80 pair of sandals because they were popular. I didn't feel very comfortable wearing grunge clothes, but I wanted to be accepted and liked by everyone else.

Jimmy.S-15:	That's not so bad. What else?
Ashley99:	I even began to listen to different music because I was embarrassed to tell anyone I listened to contemporary Christian music. I justified it by telling my friends that I thought Christian music was "boring" and "poor quality."
ChillyBilly:	Hey, IMHO, some of it is pretty lame.
MeghanM:	Yeah, but it's REALLY lame to change the music you like just to fit in with other people. ;-) But I guess you already know that, huh, Ashley?
Ashley99:	I know. But it took more than a year for me to see how stupid I was being. Then the summer before my senior year, God gave me a group of really neat Christian friends who loved me despite my grunge look. And I began to realize that "true" friends would love me for who I was. I had been trying to change myself, just to gain approval and acceptance. STUPID! God loves me for who I am, for the person He's created me to be. And true friends will love me for who I am.
TA.Host:	*Looking back, how did Teen Advisors make a difference for you in high school?*
Ashley99:	I became a Teen Advisor in my junior year. At a TA retreat, we talked about the importance of self-esteem and removing masks that hide our true self. My mask was "Miss Perfect"— but I had to learn that God loved me whether I got A's or not. And I had to learn that it was OK to do well in the classroom, too.

Leslie4U:	So did you stop wearing grunge clothes? Can I have your sandals? LOL ;0)
GinaGina:	Did you lose a lot of friends? It can be hard to change groups in high school.
Ashley99:	Well, it was hard sometimes. I remember feeling a bit persecuted when I was taunted for being "perfect," though I knew I wasn't. I was worried that the other kids would make fun of me again. But the apostle Paul tells us to rejoice when we're persecuted. And TAs taught me that God asks me not to conform to the world. Since I've grasped this concept, I've become more content with myself. Never again will I wear grunge clothes and sandals just to please people around me.
LeahLilly:	Well, I've never gone grunge, but I have gone through periods when I wrestle with what my boyfriend calls "self-pity kicks." I don't feel good enough for anyone else.
Leslie4U:	What happened, Lilly?
LeahLilly:	My family moved from South Carolina to Connecticut the summer of my freshman year. It was a real low point. I had always lived in the South, so it was a culture shock to live in a northern environment.
ChillyBilly:	What? No more chitlins? LOL See ya!
Ashley99:	Cut it out, Billy.
LeahLilly:	Anyway, I will never forget the first day of high school. I walked into the school building with a huge smile on my face, but at the end of the day, I had tears welling up in my eyes. No one knew my name—and no one really seemed to

	care. I was so lonely. All the kids in the school had grown up together in this small town, and they didn't seem interested in allowing new people to enter their tight circle. I finally got to know a few girls, but I still felt uncomfortable around them. For the longest time, I couldn't be myself around them because I was afraid they wouldn't like the real me.
Allie98:	Been there. :0(
GinaGina:	Who hasn't? What'd ya do?
LeahLilly:	The spring of my freshman year, I went out for the crew (rowing) team. I met a great group of girls who were accepting and fun to be around. Best of all, they seemed to like me for who I was. Luckily, they all shared my same moral beliefs and values. I was only with them for a year before my family moved back home, but I still keep in touch.
Tbubbles:	You must miss them. :0(
LeahLilly:	Yes, but I learned a good lesson. I realized that I needed to be myself in order to be truly happy. That's the only way to feel good about yourself. I carried that experience through my remaining years of high school, and it really helped build my confidence for life after high school! Look out world, here I come! TTFN, all.
Tbubbles:	Bye!
GinaGina:	Talk to you again soon!
Allie98:	See ya!
Ashley99:	TTFN!
Leslie4U:	What?! Is everybody going? I guess so … later.

two

Let's Chat: Is One the Loneliest Number?

TA.Host:	*Do you ever feel lonely? Do you think loneliness is a fairly common problem for teens?*
TA.ML:	I think so. Looking back on my high school years, I certainly remember going through periods of loneliness.
BlairT:	Yeah, like when your best friend is mad at you.
Allie98:	Or when your parents are so busy they don't seem to see you anymore.
LeahLilly:	I remember feeling like that when we moved. I felt so cut off from everyone.
TA.ML:	I remember a time when it was like no one, apart from my close family, wanted me around. No phone calls. No shopping trips. I felt invisible, and my feelings were hurt.
LeahLilly:	When I was going through that, I decided I had to do something. It was hard, but I started reaching out. I joined the crew team, and started inviting people over to my house. Did you try that?
TA.ML:	Not at first. My senior year was the worst. Ironically, my feelings of loneliness caused me

to depend on God and helped me prepare for college and going away.

TA.Host: *Why do you think loneliness is a big problem among teens? Is it because their parents are too busy for them? Or are kids mean to each other?*

TA.ML: Kids can be awful. They talk about each other and gossip. That's one thing Teen Advisors deals with a lot. TAs talk about not using sarcasm or gossiping behind someone's back. Those things can be destructive.

TA.Missy: I agree. Many times I can look at some kids and know that they're lonely. Other times you can tell just by the way they fit into the scheme of who's in and who's out in high school.

Allie98: Been there. :0(NO FUN!

BlairT: Well, I never had that problem. I'm lucky, I guess.

TA.Host: *Can you tell someone's lonely just by how they look?*

TA.Missy: Great question. Not always. Lonely people don't always look downtrodden and sad because they have their masks on. Loneliness can be a hard thing to tell in people.

Allie98: Yeah, there was this girl in my school who committed suicide last year. She left a note saying that nobody cared about her. The kids talked about it for weeks. Everybody said they had no idea ... but then, nobody really talked to her much. Her name was Cindy.

BlairT: I know what Missy means about this mask thing. I do that sometimes.

TA.Missy: One of my loneliest times in high school was my senior year. If you had looked at me, you would have thought that I was one of the most content persons around. I hung around with the popular people, got nominated for homecoming court, and was voted "Friendliest" in my class. On the outside, you would've thought all was well.

Allie98: And you still weren't happy? >8-0

TA.Missy: Not really. For me, a big reason why I felt lonely that year was that I was a Christian. It was also the year I wasn't dating. I had dated a guy who was not a Christian for two years, but we had stopped seeing each other between my junior and senior year of high school.

That summer I fell in love with the Lord. My conversations with my friends seemed shallow when I returned to school. The things that used to be important to me were no longer important to me—things like who you knew, what clothes you wore. While it was one of the best times in my life spiritually, it was also the loneliest time emotionally. I ate lunch by myself almost every day my senior year of high school.

TA.Host: *Is that one of the loneliest things for a high school student—eating lunch alone?*

TA.Missy: Lunch is a big deal on every high school campus, and you can tell who's in and who's

	out just by watching the seating chart. And in schools that allow students to leave campus, lunch break is a huge social event.
AprilS:	I am one of those who eats lunch alone. What advice can you give me?
TA.Missy:	If you're lonely because you're a Christian, then try to find like-minded people. Until you do, think of the times that Christ Himself felt lonely. He had all these men around Him who loved Him and said they were following Him, but when the rubber hit the road, they all fell asleep in the garden on the night before He died.
Allie98:	That's hard to imagine. They must not have loved him very much.
BlairT:	I don't know. Everybody lets you down some-times. Even family. It doesn't mean they don't love you.
TA.Missy:	I think you're right, Blair. Jesus certainly seemed to understand. Anyway, I have found comfort in that story. When you really follow Christ, the price can be walking alone, but the great thing is that you're never really alone. When Jesus said to count the cost, I think part of that cost can be loneliness.
AprilS:	But I don't WANT to be on the outside like that. And I don't understand why God would want me to be lonely, either.
TA.Missy:	Don't worry, loneliness doesn't last forever. The best way to cure sadness or loneliness is to look for ways to serve others. Look for those in life who have it harder than you do and reach

	out to them. When you focus on being there for other people, it curbs your desire to feel sorry for yourself.
RayGun:	I'm a senior in high school, and for the past three years I have had many friends with the same beliefs as me. But the last few months have been totally different because my friends, who used to believe that drinking was wrong, have all started to drink. Even some of my strong Christian friends have started to drink and experiment with drugs.
Dan0831:	It hurts when your friends switch paths and lose their love for Christ. It bothers me to hear the guys talking about going to a party and getting drunk. But then I say to myself, "Even though they know it's wrong, they do it anyway just to fit in." I wish I could tell all of them to get a backbone and not give in to what everybody else is doing. But I don't blame God for what is going wrong. I just keep doing what I know is right.
Chris2fer:	My first year of high school I didn't know many people. Plus I was shy. It wasn't until the second month of school that I started to actually make friends. Teen Advisors helped. At a TA retreat I heard about the masks we all wear. I wasn't sure about taking off my mask and just being myself, but when I did, I realized that it wasn't too bad at all. It seemed that I could just be myself, and that was fine with everyone.
TA.Missy:	I'm glad it helped you, Chris. :0)
Chris2fer:	It really did. After that retreat, I wasn't embar-

rassed to walk up to someone and have a conversation. Since then, I've made many new friends, and I no longer feel lonely. I learned that people really like me more when I'm just being myself. NO FEAR. No masks.

TA.Host:	*That's great, Chris. Anyone else have an experience they want to talk about?*
Caleb42:	Loneliness started for me in ninth grade. I'm homeschooled, and then my family changed churches. Consequently, I had no friends. Then I got involved in a bad relationship with a girl. Emotionally, she made me feel like I could trust her with my struggles, but then my confidences got passed around. I thought about suicide.
BlairT:	Suicide? :0(How old were you?
Caleb42:	Fourteen.
Allie98:	Wow. Just like Cindy.
BlairT:	What kept you from committing suicide?
Caleb42:	I thought about it for a long time, but I never had the guts to do it. Now I know that God kept me safe for a reason. Suicide is never the answer. It's awful for everyone involved.
Allie98:	Yeah. I saw Cindy's mom the other day. It's been two years, but she still cried when I talked about her. They miss her so much. I would NEVER put my parents through that.
BlairT:	What advice can you give?
Caleb42:	Life may look bad, but things are going to get better. God will pull you through, even when you aren't relying on Him the way you should.

	No matter how bad it gets, suicide is never the solution.
BlairT:	Was there a section of the Bible that helped you get through this difficult time?
Caleb42:	Philippians 4 has been one of my favorites: I can do all things through Christ who strengthens me. I've learned to be content in all situations. When I know things aren't that great, I can get through this.
TA.Host:	*Let's talk about dealing with depression.*
Nick22:	If you're depressed, time by itself won't get rid of depression. You have to help yourself out of the situation by finding something fun to do. Having fun is one of the best remedies for depression.
Chris2fer:	Like playing basketball!
BlairT:	Or invite a few friends over to watch videos.
Nick22:	Yeah, like a comedy. Personally, I like to be around other people who are laughing. It's hard for me to stay depressed in a roomful of fun. Going to get something to eat, bowling, or seeing a movie with a friend is a good way to snap out of it.
BigBrian:	Exercise is another good way to make you happy.
AprilS:	Yes, but I'm still lonely.
BigBrian:	You won't be lonely with God in your life. He'll be your friend. Besides, even popular people experience loneliness. Even tho they might hide it better.
BlairT:	Brian's right, April.

GinaGina:	I'm one of those who hid my feelings well. I remember one Tuesday night at a Bible study. I was frustrated and not knowing what was going on. I could be with people and still feel alone. I didn't understand how I could feel alone with people around talking to me.
LeslieB:	That's exactly how I feel sometimes! :-]~
GinaGina:	When I told Missy how I felt, she started laughing. She reminded me that God created me as a unique person, and there is no else like me. "The longer you try to be like everyone, the more miserable you'll be," she said. Her answer helped me get over this, and it's advice you can take to heart as well.
TA.Host:	*Good discussion, everyone. Come back tomorrow for our next topic! We talked about what to do when we don't like what's going on inside. Next we'll discuss how it feels when you don't like what's on the OUTSIDE!*

three

Let's Chat: Living With the Body God Gave You

TA.Host:	*OK, give us the scoop. How do you feel about how you look? If you could change something about your body, would you?*
EarlyBloom:	I WOULD! My looks have caused me most of my worry. I'm only five feet tall, and I'm not necessarily fat, but my shortness makes me look as if I weigh much more than I really do.
SlimSue:	At least if you're short you don't stick out too much. I'm taller than all the guys in my class!
StiltBoy:	Well, my name says it all. Being tall is nothing compared to being short! I'm shorter than all the girls! :-{
EarlyBloom:	Short is bad enough, but I'm ALSO much bigger on top than most girls my age. I hate being big-busted! I bloomed before anyone else in my elementary school, and it seems as if I just never stopped.
JulieK:	Uh … how big are you?
EarlyBloom:	Let's just say girls who complain because they are a B-cup have no idea what they are talking about! You have no idea how much it hurts to walk down the school hall and hear the boys

	make rude comments. Last summer at a family gathering my uncle started cracking jokes about how I'm bigger than my twenty-three-year-old cousin—and I'm only thirteen!
JulieK:	Yeah, that would be embarrassing. So is "birdlegs," which is MY family's pet nickname. (Why do people who are supposed to love you SAY things like that?!) :0(
PhoeBD:	Birdlegs? I wish! I'm sixteen, and only 5'2" and 140 pounds. That may not seem too bad, but when I look in the mirror it's horrible! I have this "athlete" tag on me. You see, I've played soccer all my life against girls who are skinnier, smaller, and a lot more in shape than me. My legs are HUGE, and while they are 99 percent muscle, I think everyone sees them as just fat. My stomach is larger than I'd like it to be, but I've tried everything, and it won't get flatter.
StiltBoy:	I know what you mean about trying everything. I even stuffed my shoes with socks to make me taller. Then the guys found out in gym. I was so embarrassed, I pretended I was sick so I didn't have to go to school the next day.
TA.Host:	*Have you tried talking with your parents?*
PhoeBD:	I've asked my parents not to pester me with their remarks. As long as I know that I am doing the best I can to take care of myself, I am OK, but sometimes I just don't have time to go to the gym or to go running. Although

it's pretty impossible, my eyes see a bigger me every day! All I can do about it is tell myself I look fine and listen to the compliments. I'm still working on accepting myself as I am.

CassandraM: I have acne. How am I supposed to accept this mess?! Help! =8>o

TA.Missy: My complexion was awful in junior high. I used to cry all the time. I had to go to the dermatologist regularly. I prayed that my complexion would be clear, and it eventually got better.

CassandraM: You prayed the pimples away? :-}

TA.Missy: Hang in there. Just remember that it probably won't always be like this. It's bad now, but it'll get better. God isn't finished with you.

Spencer06: Missy's right. In grade school, I was the tallest and thinnest in all of my classes. To make things worse, I had a sensitive personality. I was the kid the whole class picked on. I never got invited to parties, and even though I was good at sports, my coaches ignored me. I worked hard, played hard, and strove to do my best— but I was too quiet.

CassandraM: Sounds like things were pretty rough. When did things start to turn around for you?

Spencer06: Teen Advisors helped me develop my leadership skills and introduced me to a group of people who saw past my outer shell and noticed my hard work, determination, kindness, compassion, and love. It really helped me to discover that "God does not make junk." Knowing that Christ dwells in me has also made a vast difference in how I view myself—

	and hence how others see me. I was selected as the Athlete of the Year for my senior class—and I'll be going to college on a scholarship.
CassandraM:	You sure turned things around.
Spencer06:	My advice on those with a poor body image? Hang in there. Things may not change overnight, but I promise that the Lord will bless those who fear Him and seek His will. He did it for me, and He can do it for you. Be confident in yourself and your abilities. Ask God to use you and bless you as you serve Him. Remember to live for an audience of One (God) and to serve Him with all you have. He will bless you beyond what others and yourself can imagine.
TA.Host:	*Anyone else?*
MaryMary:	I have a problem with how I look, too. Sometimes it's better than others, but when it's bad, it's really bad. I've even missed school and church because I felt so bad about my looks.
CassandraM:	Do you have acne?
MaryMary:	The reasons I feel inadequate have changed over the years. My dad got laid off and we didn't have money for clothes. Then I got heavier and my face started breaking out. None of the problems are big in and of them-selves, but in my mind they are giant. It's hard for me to make friends, and sometimes I'm not very nice to my family.
PhoeBD:	It can be hard when your family keeps getting

GinnyB: on you about your weight. And just as hard not to worry about what other people think of you. Hang in there! :o)

GinnyB: I like how I look. But I guess it can be hard if you're not popular—isn't that every teenager's dream in life?

SoccerPaul: The trouble is, being popular can change in a minute. In junior high I hung out with some popular people, was known as one of the best dudes on the soccer team, and I even dated a pretty girl. But then everything changed—and it happened so fast!

GinnyB: What happened?

SoccerPaul: The popular kids began making fun of me. One summer in junior high I had a surgery that left a pretty nasty scar on the side of my face. They enjoyed making snide comments about it. I laughed along, even though their words tore me up on the inside. But I couldn't let it show.

GinnyB: Did it get better in high school?

SoccerPaul: You would think so, but the first day of high school was another dose of reality. I remember making mental notes of who was going to be popular so I could befriend those people. I was a miserable failure. I just couldn't fit in.

GinnyB: How come? :^(

SoccerPaul: I was insecure. I thought it was evident to everyone that I was from the other side of the tracks. They were rich, and my family was barely making it. So I didn't say anything to anyone. My high school years would have been

	a disaster, but a girl talked me into joining Teen Advisors. Talk about doing wonders for my self-esteem! Teen Advisors provided me with friends to hang out with, to eat lunch with, and to acknowledge in the halls. I suddenly had a group of friends who were more family than anything.
GinnyB:	So that's the answer—join Teen Advisors.
SoccerPaul:	It really helped me. Of course, not everyone goes to a high school that has Teen Advisors. If that's your situation, then find other Christians at your school. Most of all, you need to make friends with the Lord Jesus Christ. He became my friend one night during my sophomore year—and He is the source of all healing.
PhoeBD:	It sounds like you're saying that if you are just a Christian, you won't have any more problems. That can't be true!
SoccerPaul:	That's not what I meant. Even after becoming a Christian, I continued to strive after popularity in many ways. There were times when my self-image didn't stem from God—it stemmed from how others perceived me. I still valued myself according to how others valued me.
GinnyB:	So I should know that ...
SoccerPaul:	Friends will fail you, and you'll probably fail yourself a few times, but God will never fail you. I have learned that the more confidence I have in Christ, the more secure I am around people. And the more secure I am around people, the more I'll be able to make friends.

TA.Host:	*Let's go back to the original subject. What do people say that makes it easier—or harder—to be comfortable with how God made you?*
PhoeBD:	It's hard to take it serious when someone says something to make me feel better. I put myself down a lot, even when someone tells me I am pretty. When I hear a compliment, I say, "Well, that's your opinion," or, "I don't know about that." I should just say thanks and go on, but it's not easy.
EarlyBloom:	The worst is when the guys tease me. Some of my friends try to make me feel better by saying, "I wish I had your problem." But I would switch with them in a minute!
PhoeBD:	Even my parents haven't been very helpful, I'm afraid. They tell me every time I put on a bathing suit or anything remotely tight that I need to start running more often. I don't like the negative comments. Who would? So I just try to tell myself that God made me—for a reason. He knew what He was doing when He created me.
TA.Host:	*Hold that thought, Phoebe! Lots of young women struggle with their weight—and some even do dangerous things to keep their weight down. Come and join us in the next room.*

four

Girl's Chat: The Secret Struggle of Eating Disorders

TA.Host:	*We hear a lot on the news about eating disorders like bulimia and anorexia, but it's hard to believe that there are that many who would actually get caught up in it. In a class of one hundred girls, how many would you say are battling some type of eating disorder?*
TA.Missy:	I would say one out of three.
BluJean:	Every time I look at *Seventeen*, I worry about my weight and what I eat. Is this normal?
MaryBeth5:	I don't know about "normal," but you're not alone! It's different for everyone.
Janey18:	I started dieting when I was eight because my brother teased me about "thunder thighs."
TrishA!:	I started working out when I was twelve because I didn't want to be heavy like my mom … :0(
TA.Host:	*There's a big difference between eating well and exercising to stay healthy and developing an eating disorder. Does anyone here know someone who crossed that line?*
MaryBeth5:	I do. For me, it started because I was very self-conscious, always worrying about adding a

	pound or if someone would notice a zit on my face. Those feelings led to my eating disorder.
TrishA!:	What happened?
MaryBeth5:	When I was alone in my bedroom, I would say over and over, "You are fat, you are fat. If you could just lose a little more weight, you would be a much better person."
CathiK:	You were pretty hard on yourself. So what did you do?
MaryBeth5:	Actually, I was surprised how easy it was to lose weight if I really wanted to. I did become thin—all the way to ninety pounds. I was horribly skinny, but even when I weighed ninety pounds, I thought I could still lose a little bit more.
SuzieQ:	Didn't your parents notice?
MaryBeth5:	Sure, they tried to talk to me. They saw that I was skipping breakfast and picking at dinner. They didn't realize I was also throwing away my lunch.
Jenna16:	What did they do? Were they mad?
MaryBeth5:	They are both doctors, and knew what was going on. They scared me with their statistics, and reminded me that I could ruin my reproductive organs and heart. I would also be more susceptible to diseases.
CathiK:	How long ago did this happen?
MaryBeth5:	About four years ago, and I'm still working on getting over this. Today, I am a cross-country runner who is surrounded by beautiful girls at school. (Can you tell I still feel self-conscious?)
PhoeBD:	That must keep the extra weight off!

MaryBeth5:	Well, yes and no. As a runner, I need certain vitamins to perform, and during the last cross-country season, I completely bottomed out. I had no energy to run, and I did not want to believe I wasn't giving myself enough food. My body began to eat away at my body, and let me tell you, when it reached that point, my eating disorder was very dangerous.
Jenna16:	Scary! :-o
MaryBeth5:	I started counseling, and I've learned that it will be hard to get back completely to normal. I'm working on boosting my self-image, reminding myself how beautiful God made me.
BrittanE:	It's hard to remember that sometimes. I'm just five feet tall, so I've always worried about my weight. I matured in sixth grade, and I have a large bust. You can't believe how many comments I've heard about my breasts! Then in the eighth grade, a girl told me that when she lost a lot of weight, her chest size shrunk. So I began to starve myself.
EarlyBloom:	Did it work?
BrittanE:	I lost weight all right. But when I realized that I had to eat, I couldn't get the food down. My parents started making me take vitamins to give me an appetite, but they didn't work. What had started out as something to make my chest smaller had turned into something I couldn't control by myself anymore.
Jenna16:	Was it hard to tell your parents?
BrittanE:	Yes, but God helped me. Anyone who thinks she might have an eating disorder MUST find

some adult who can help—a parent, teacher, pastor, someone. Friends can help to some extent, but not the same as adults. And always ask God for help, since He can get you through what no one else can.

TA.Host: *Does anyone else have a story to share?*

MeghanR: My eating disorder started when I ate lunch with a friend who was into healthy eating. She kept counting calories and fat grams, so I started doing the same thing—but I took it one step farther. If anything had over two grams of fat, I wouldn't pour the dressing on my salad. If I did eat, then I had to get rid of the calories and fat by exercising or throwing up.

EarlyBloom: Yuck!!!

MeghanR: It wasn't long before I felt horrible just eating a regular meal. If I ate "bad" foods one day, then I got into the worst mood. When I threw it up, I felt bad and cried a lot. The only time I felt good was when I didn't eat anything all day. But then I felt real shaky and dizzy.

Jenna16: Do you need to get help?

MeghanR: I know I need help, but I'm not ready because I'm not skinny enough yet. I *used* to be a real happy person, but now I'm always depressed. I feel very confused all the time.

BrittanE: Maybe you should talk to your parents.

MeghanR: I can't talk to my parents, and I'm afraid that if I tell my friends, then they'll tell *their* friends, and I won't be known as Meghan but as that girl with an eating disorder. I don't want that at all! I'm also afraid that people at school won't like me. Anytime anyone whispers, I think they're talking about me. I'm so paranoid.

TA.Host: *But couldn't your parents help you?*

MeghanR: Not only would that be totally embarrassing, but I know my parents would bug me about eating, and that will take all my control away. That's the biggest part of an eating disorder—CONTROL. I've got to have it. Plus, I don't want my parents to know because I'm afraid they'll blame themselves, and it's not their fault at all. They've been so great! They tell me I'm beautiful, and they love me even when I'm not lovable. I feel guilty and ashamed. I'm afraid people will think I'm a freak. I want it to go away but it won't.

BrittanE: It sounds like your parents love you a lot. Even if you tell them about your problem, they'll still love you. My parents never gave up on me—and yours will do the same for you.

TA.Host: *BrittanE is right. If you can't talk to your parents, though, find some adult you can talk to. Meghan, we're going to be praying for you. But for the rest of the people online, maybe you recognize yourself in these girls' stories. If so, it's important that you get help, too. Talk to a teacher, a school counselor, or your pastor. If you know someone who has an eating disorder, pray for her and encourage her to get help. Does anyone else have a story?*

TA.ML:	Up until my senior year of high school, I always felt comfortable with my appearance. I never worried about my weight. But then during my senior year, I put on a little bit of weight, and I felt horrible about it.
Tina@12:	How much extra weight?
TA.ML:	Not much. Ten pounds, maybe. I remember asking my boyfriend about it, asking what I should do if I got up to 135 pounds. I remember him saying, "Don't get much bigger than that."
EarlyBloom:	Did you?
TA.ML:	I passed that mark and tried to get the weight off, but it didn't happen. I worried, but I didn't panic until I went to college and gained ten *more* pounds.
Jenna16:	Oh, no! How embarrassing! :0(
TA.ML:	It was a vicious cycle. The truth is, my body size is not naturally small. But that's all I saw in the fashion magazines and the movies and TV shows. Being thin is what our society tells us we have to be. It's what guys tell girls they should be like. I can remember hearing guys saying in high school, "Hey, look at that fat girl," when her hips were just a little big. The minute I heard a guy say that, I thought, *If he says it about her, he'll say it about me.*
Tina@12:	What were some of the things you did to try to lose weight?
TA.ML:	I did some stupid things. My best friend and I thought it was funny to buy a half-gallon of ice cream and eat it all in one night. Then, we

would do a hundred push-ups and a hundred sit-ups and drink a gallon of water. We thought the exercise and water would cancel the calories out. My senior year, I read a story in *Seventeen* magazine about a girl who was taking laxatives for her eating disorder. That story put a lot of ideas in my head, and I tried laxatives.

NatashaJ: Did the laxatives work?

TA.ML: I could eat a meal and take a laxative, and in a matter of a few hours, that meal passed right through me. That was hard on my body, though, and it wasn't healthy at all.

TA.Missy: I can attest to that. I once lived with three roommates who had eating disorders. I could never get my roommates to admit they had eating disorders. They thought an eating disorder was sticking your finger down your throat or massively eating a lot of food. That's not entirely true. Being obsessed with your weight can be as much of a disorder.

EarlyBloom: What do you mean?

TA.Missy: Too many girls are obsessed with comparing their bodies and different body parts with others. "Oh, gosh. Her legs are so much longer and thinner than mine." Or, "Her hair is so much straighter than mine. I hate my hair." Or, "Look at her figure. She looks like Demi Moore."

BluJean: You know someone who looks like Demi Moore?

TA.Missy: You're missing the point. This type of thinking is where eating disorders start. They plant little

	seeds in their minds about their weight, and when they suddenly sprout up, they become obsessed. And they have a full-blown eating disorder. Like this one girl who recently told me, "Missy, I think about being skinny all the time. I don't want to wait. I want to be skinny right now."
NatashaJ:	How overweight was this girl?
TA.Missy:	She was healthy. She wasn't overweight. God didn't create everyone's body to look like Barbie. Barbie isn't a real person. It all comes back to comparison. Maybe a boyfriend says your butt's getting fat. Or a mom puts you on a diet when you're going into adolescence and your body is changing and maturing. But the truth is, it's natural to add some body fat.
BluJean:	Natural to be FAT?
TA.Missy:	Women need a certain level of body fat for when they want to have babies later in life.
Mallory12:	My pressure to stay slim actually comes from my family. My mother is a ballet dancer, and so are my sisters and my cousin. Much of our lives has revolved around ballet. I've always been surrounded by their long torsos and long, thin legs. Me, this little five-foot, solidly built girl who would give anything to be five foot, eight inches tall and 110 pounds—just like my mom.
BluJean:	Wow! Talk about pressure!
TA.Missy:	What did you do?
Mallory12:	I started trying to make myself into the dancer's mold. I knew that I could never be tall, but I could be *skinny*. So I dieted and

	dieted and dieted. I wanted to be a famous dancer one day, and I knew better than others that a dancer's career revolves around what she looks like. All I did was watch the food that I ate. My bathroom scale became my best friend. When the weight didn't come off like I wanted, I started taking diet pills and making myself throw up.
MaryKate:	You sound like you went off the deep end. What happened?
Mallory12:	Slowly, I realized that I could never change my five-foot squat frame. Nor could I reduce the size of my quads by obsessively questioning everything I ate. I finally faced that my dream to dance on stage was not realistic. So I quit dancing. I know my mother was disappointed, but she supported me through it all, and she still does.
MaryKate:	Were you able to kick your eating disorder?
Mallory12:	It's an ongoing battle. I love the person that I am inside my head, but a lot of times the person on the outside doesn't let that inner person show. I have a feeling that one day I will find a happy medium, but I'm still waiting. In the meantime, I've found other activities—like pottery and soccer—that make me feel better about myself.
TA.Host:	*What should Mallory and others do to get a grip on their eating disorders?*
TA.Missy:	Accountability is IMPORTANT! Ask yourself if you're being honest with your parents about

	whether you're really eating or not. I think a big fruit of wrong self-image is lying. You lie to cover up your actions. So number one, you have to stop lying. What is going on in your life is not normal. It's not right.
BrittanE:	Counseling really helped me. I was able to trace the problem back to its start. That made it easier to prevent it happening again.
MaryKate:	My parents would freak out, so I can't go to them.
TA.Missy:	Well, they might. One girl told me her father thought her eating disorder was a ruse to get attention. He was a prominent man in our community. He couldn't imagine his daughter having an eating disorder. But your parents might surprise you. Think about going to them.
NatashaJ:	Can't you just start eating more?
TA.Missy:	It's not that easy. Sometimes it helps to set goals for yourself. I had a roommate with a severe eating disorder. She would wake up in the morning, run for five miles, swim seventy laps, and then go to school. She was probably 5'7" and weighed 115 pounds—built like a rail. She would never eat meat of any kind. We talked about it, and she told me that she wanted to get to a place that was a little more normal, so I helped her set a goal. We decided that her first goal was to eat a piece of fish before the end of summer. She did eat fish about three times. For her, that was an accomplishment.

NatashaJ:	What did you say that helped her?
TA.Missy:	A lot of it was saying, "Jennie, I want you to know that I love you unconditionally and that I accept you where you are, but I can't accept that what you are doing is right." From that, Jennie always knew that no matter how things got, no matter what she was doing to herself, that I loved her and I was running alongside her as her friend. She even said that because we could talk so openly about it, she could tell she was getting better in her thinking.
TA.Host:	*Should Jennie have sought professional help?*
TA.Missy:	For some, eating disorders are like a secret kind of sin—there is a lot of shame and guilt over it. So it's hard for people to talk about. You can't force someone to get help before they are ready. Obviously, my roommate had a severe problem. You don't exercise that much and eat so little and not say there's something wrong with this picture.
TA.Host:	*Do you think there is any connection between overcoming eating disorders and spiritual growth?*
TA.Anne:	I do. I continue to struggle with an eating disorder. It started in college. Ever heard of the "Freshman Fifteen"? Well, that was me. I did make some great friends at college, though, including my roommate, who is still my best friend today. We both love Christ and did a great job of encouraging each other. Yet we

were both very obsessed with the way we looked, which was constantly fed by our complaints each time we got dressed in the morning. Our critical comments seemed so harmless, yet it would put a very negative attitude on our day. More importantly, that gave Satan the biggest foothold into our weaknesses.

MaryKate: ??? What do you mean by that? What does Satan have to do with this?! 8^0

TA.Anne: Because our focus was on ourselves and not on God, my roommate and I felt so horribly about ourselves. We grumbled, we complained, then we started some bad habits together. And Satan used these things to draw us farther and farther from God.

NatashaJ: You must have been pretty unhappy. Did you try to do anything about your problem?

TA.Anne: I decided to attend an eating disorder seminar offered at my school, but I couldn't go just for myself. I decided to accompany a friend who was into serious eating problems, but deep down, I knew I was going out of fear that I had a problem.

EarlyBloom: Did it help?

TA.Anne: Unfortunately, the seminar was led by people who were new to the subject. A tiny, slim girl told us how awful her experience was. All I could focus on was how skinny she was and how wonderful I would feel when I was her size. She showed us how she lost weight—and I left that seminar not thinking about my eating disorder, but about her "weight loss tips."

It just fueled my imagination with ideas. It was hard to listen to the horrible effects of what they did when they were standing before me in a size 4.

NatashaJ: Did anyone catch on?

TA.Anne: Fortunately, someone noticed my problem and told me I should either talk to someone or tell my parents. I chose the former because I didn't want my parents to know. My friend not only scared me to death, but she taught me a lot. Then I saw a news special on eating disorders, and they showed an eighty-pound girl with knees like softballs who had to be carried everywhere. Still, she said she felt fat. I watched in amazement and wondered, "How in the world could she say that?"

Jenna16: Did you relate to that girl?

TA.Anne: Not until the reporter started reading from this girl's journal. I listened as she described feeling like the fattest person in the room. She wrote of how she only wanted to lose a little more weight—then her life would be so much happier. When I heard that, I realized that her feelings were no different than mine. Sure, she was fifty or sixty pounds lighter than me and facing death, but I was headed down the same road.

MaryKate: What did you learn from all this?

TA.Anne: Most of all, I've learned to get closer to God, and to rely upon His protection. It's been about four years, and I still pray every day for Christ to help me fight this disease. I have also relied a lot on Psalm 139:14: "I praise you because I am fearfully and wonderfully made; your works are wonderful, I know that full well." This Scripture tells me that I was designed exactly the way Christ wants me to be, and that I have no right to harm my body because it does not belong to me. I often think of how it makes God feel when He hears me criticize something He takes such pride in.

Andrea99: I have some friends who are obsessed with their weight. What are some warning signs that they might have a disorder?

TA.Anne: Using any type of diet pill is a bad sign. They may seem harmless, but they are not. Some other signs are: frequent visits to the bathroom after meals, watery eyes (from gagging), scrapes on the knuckles (from teeth scraping the hand as a person gags herself), not eating meals but picking at other people's food, leaving around meal times, always being busy during meals, or sleeping during meals. Compulsive exercising or talking about food or weight are other important signs.

Andrea99: Did anyone notice these signs about you?

TA.Anne: No! I wish someone had. If you think you have an eating disorder, seek help! Prayer is also a great way to start dealing with your problem.

TA.Host: *What can parents do if they think their child has an eating disorder?*

TA.Anne: Sadly, there is not much you can do until your child realizes she has a problem. A good way to help your child's self-esteem would be to give her positive reinforcement: emphasize her gifts, talents, inner beauty, and character qualities rather than her appearance and performance. Don't make snide remarks about her weight. Let her know it is not her "outside" that you love or are proud of, but rather her "inside." Love her unconditionally.

TA.Host: *What would you say is the most important distinction between someone who tries to lose weight in a healthy way and someone with an eating disorder?*

MissMindy: I think a lot of it has to do with WHY you want to lose the weight. A lot of the problem is fear, plain and simple. I remember going on the TA's spring beach retreat was *such* a source of fear for me. I took my diet pills with me to the retreat. It wasn't long before I felt ashamed to be at a retreat promoting being drug-free and being with God when I had the tools of the devil in my backpack. That beach retreat was a good reality check, and even though it's been hard, I haven't taken a diet pill since then. *And man, am I proud of that!* My head has been such a battleground.

Jenna16: What do you mean?

MissMindy: I can hear two voices—the devil and the Holy Spirit. I hear "You're beautiful," and then I hear, "No, you're not. You're fat." Those thoughts kill me, but when I finally got it through my thick skull that the latter voice was lying, I was OK. I can fight bad thoughts now, and so can you. Identify who it is in your head saying the negative and positive things, and learn to fight the negative. The Word of God is the best weapon for any battle. Also, confide in someone and don't carry your burden alone.

TA.Host: *Wow! We've talked about some issues here that are really a matter of life and death. The next couple of topics are just as important—what you decide to do with these issues is also a matter of life and death. Stay with us!*

five

Let's Chat: Is It Ever OK to Drink?

TA.Host:	*I've heard that Teen Advisors sign one-year contracts not to drink. Why? And do they follow through?*
TA.ML:	TAs sign the contract for several different reasons. Clearly, the biggest reason is because it's illegal for teens to drink. But drinking can also lead to sinful behavior and cause accidents. Signing a contract like this is one way that we can be real role models when we go and speak in classrooms.
Philberry:	But don't you feel pressured to drink when you're with your friends?
TA.ML:	Actually, I signed the contract and became a Teen Advisor because I needed the accountability from among my friends. Even more than that, I needed the assurance that I was part of something that was bigger than me.
NickAtNite:	What's the big deal? So I have a beer with my friends once in a while!
TA.Jen:	Liquor is dangerous. And when you're drinking, your sense of right and wrong and

	your decision-making process are not as clear as they should be.
GinaGina:	Hello again! Jen is right. I'm not a Christian or anything, but I don't drink. Two kids in my class were killed last year in a drunk driving accident. They ran a train crossing. I can't believe anyone would be that dumb.
TA.Jen:	I'm sorry that happened, Gina. The truth is, lots of people have been killed or hurt badly as a result of drinking alcohol. Think about your friends who've drunk and how stupid they acted. Think about your friends who got real sick after drinking.
NickAtNite:	But nobody gets drunk on one beer!
GinaGina:	Are you kidding? 8^0 Alcohol is alcohol!
TA.Jen:	The fact is, I can't think of one good reason for drinking, especially before the legal age limit. The younger you start, the more likely it will lead to other things. If you start drinking at fifteen, you may start smoking pot at seventeen and doing other drugs at eighteen!
SophSam:	I hear some of the upperclassmen are going out drinking after the big homecoming game. My older brother says it's no big deal, and I'm inclined to agree with him.
TA.ML:	How old is he?
SophSam:	He's a senior.
TA.ML:	So legally he's still not old enough to drink. That's a big deal. Drinking is not going to win you friends in the long run.
SophSam:	Have you ever had a drink, ML?

NickAtNite:	Yeah, IMHO, she probably doesn't know what she's missing.
TA.ML:	Yes, I do … in fact, it's one of the reasons I feel so strongly about this issue. I can speak out of experience.
SophSam:	Really? What happened?
TA.ML:	When I was a sophomore in high school, there was a VIP program at school, which was the drug and alcohol-free group before Teen Advisors started at my school. Well, this VIP group went on a ski trip, and a bunch of kids smuggled beer on the trip. It was a big deal that everybody drink some, and so I drank, too.
NickAtNite:	Party!
TA.ML:	No. When I got back home and my parents and the school found out, I had to make a public apology and lose my office. It was really embarrassing. I felt kind of wimpy to let my parents down and let God down.
SophSam:	Oh, don't be so down on yourself. So why did you get involved with TA, since the other group didn't work for you?
TA.ML:	Well, I was involved in VIP my freshman year. I wasn't mature enough then to make a real commitment. But in my junior year, I signed a TA contract and stuck with it throughout high school. That was a real empowering thing for me.
TA.Jen:	Let me jump in here. I, too, kept my TA contract throughout high school, and when I went to the University of Alabama—a very large

	state school—I really relied on what I learned in Teen Advisors.
NickAtNite:	You're kidding! Everybody drinks in college. And it's even legal for some of them!
TA.Jen:	It may be legal for some—but it's still not smart. Shortly after I arrived on campus, I pledged a sorority where I thought there would be lots of people just like me—you know, people who knew how to go out and have a good time without drinking.
GinaGina:	Wow! I didn't know they have sororities like that.
TA.Jen:	Well, I wanted to be sure before I joined. So one night at a pledge retreat, we had a "unity circle." Everyone shared some things about themselves. When it was my turn to talk, my heart was beating real fast.
SophSam:	What happened?
TA.Jen:	Somehow I got the courage to say: "I want to let you know that I don't drink. I made this decision a long time ago. I still like to go out and have a good time and do fun things, but the only difference is I don't drink. I don't want you to be intimidated by that, and I won't be judging you at all. At the same time, I don't want you to think that I'm weird. I just want you to know that not drinking is part of me."
NickAtNite:	Wow, you must have blown their minds! >8-)
TA.Jen:	It was a scary feeling. These were girls who didn't know me and had no reason to think that I was cool or cute. But do you know what

	happened after that unity circle broke up? I had three other girls come up to me, and each one whispered the same thing: "I don't want to drink either, but I was too chicken to say anything."
SophSam:	So what did you do when they had parties? Go up to your room and study?
MarGee:	Hello everyone! Thought I'd drop in and chat awhile.
TA.Jen:	Hello, MarGee. Glad you could join us. Well, at my sorority there were a lot of girls who bet that it would only take a few weeks before I'd start drinking. But when the months passed by and I still hadn't had a drink, they saw my commitment was real.
NickAtNite:	I can just hear it now. "Gingerale Jen." ;-)
TA.Jen:	I did get teased sometimes. But even my sisters who drank would keep me accountable. I would go to fraternity parties and talk to others with a glass of water in my hand. When I was holding a cup that wasn't see-through, friends would come up to me and say, "Jennifer, what are you doing?" And they'd always take my cup.
TA.Missy:	You mean they didn't want you to drink?
SophSam:	Ah, they just wanted to win their bet.
TA.Jen:	No, I think that in their own way they respected me. It continued like that through college. They would always be so concerned, which was amazing to me. I think they wanted me to be the person who they could count on to be sober. Then I'd have friends come to me

and say: "Jennifer, I'm not going to drink tonight. Is it OK if I hang out with you?" Or, "I think it's neat you're not drinking. I wish I could be like you." Or, "Jennifer, help me out. I don't want to get drunk."

GinaGina: But why would you want to spend so much time with people who drank if you don't drink?

TA.Jen: I wanted to make a difference, to be a good example to them, too. And it worked. Slowly but surely, they'd start coming to my dorm room at night, confiding in me and asking me to pray for them. I even started a Bible study in the house. By the time my junior year rolled around, I had several girls in my sorority house—the same ones who I was afraid three years earlier were going to reject me—ask me to run for president of the sorority. Suddenly, they were looking at me to represent them. I was very moved by that.

TA.Missy: Did you win? Inquiring minds want to know.

TA.Jen: I decided not to run for president. Instead I was voted Standards Chairman, which was the person in the house who was in charge of reprimanding or correcting people when their social behavior got out of line. Usually, the sorority picked someone who would be kind of lax or understanding—certainly not someone who had decided not to drink or have premarital sex.

MarGee: But don't you think it would have been better to have a little fun in the beginning, and go straight later on? I mean, it must have been

	boring to have to be Miss Goody Two Shoes all the time!
TA.Jen:	I don't agree, MarGee. By taking a stand early—the first week, in fact—I never had to take a stand again. All along, I had been afraid that these people would resent me or not be friends with me because I was different. But none of that happened. It was harder for those who drank and slept around, and later decided to turn their lives around. They had been viewed as party girls, so it was very difficult to change their reputations.
JoshOOa:	I agree with Jen. It's important to take a stand early. You need to think ahead and choose your behavior. If you don't think about whether you'll drink in advance, you'll probably go with the majority's decision. And that's definitely NOT cool.
Philberry:	I don't know ... you see a group of guys huddled around a bonfire after a game, laughing and talking with cheerleaders. It looks pretty cool to me. Real macho.
JoshOOa:	No way. It's way more macho NOT to drink.
SophSam:	But my brother and his friends are going drinking after the game. What should I do? I don't want to hang by myself.
TomTunes:	Just as you know the kids who are going to drink, you have a pretty good idea who *isn't* going to drink. Decide what you're going to do with your sober friends. Good luck.

TA.Host:	*Thanks for your insights on teenage drinking. We know that lots of teenagers have easy access to alcohol at home because their own parents drink, sometimes a lot. Has anyone in this Chat Room lived with an alcoholic parent?*
Dan0831:	That would be me. I grew up in a home of alcoholic parents.

TA.Host:	*Do you feel comfortable talking about it?*
Dan0831:	Yes, because it's something our family has taken steps to deal with. But it took a while for us to get honest with ourselves. Being honest is very important. With children of alcoholics, it's hard to be honest with what's going on.
MarGee:	What do you mean, be honest? Isn't it obvious what's going on?
Dan0831:	Sometimes you see something going on but just don't talk about it. I know I felt a lot of blame for the situation. It wasn't until I learned that Mom had been sexually abused as a kid and used drinking as a way to cope that I saw it wasn't my fault.

TA.Host:	*What was a typical day in your household?*
Dan0831:	After I came home from school, Mom would start drinking. Miller Light. She'd put one away after another and then conk out.
TA.ML:	How awful! :-(That must have been hard on you.
Dan0831:	You get used to it, I guess. In the morning, she'd wake up groggy. I'd help her get going in the morning, but I had to get myself ready for

	school. I did learn a lot of responsibility that way.
MarGee:	Yeah, my father drank a lot after Mom left, too. Fortunately, it didn't last. He got help.
Dan0831:	You're lucky. I wasn't old enough—I think I was ten—to know how to get help for Mom. She tried to commit suicide when I was still in elementary school. She tried to OD on Valium. It took years before she got any help, and there's still a lot of pain in our family today. That's one of the aftereffects of drinking.
TA.Host:	*Did anyone grow up in a household where their parents didn't drink at all?*
Adrienne3:	I did. The two main factors that kept me from using alcohol or drugs were my parents and the Lord.
TA.Missy:	Why your parents?
Adrienne3:	They are Christians, and taught me from the time I was little that my body is the temple of the Lord and that drinking would ruin it. Drinking would also be a sin for me. That's why I don't do it.
Carlos19:	Listen to your mother … ;-)
JoshOOa:	I have a sister seven years older than me. She started drinking in high school. It got worse. Sometimes she wouldn't come home, and my sister became very distant and experienced lots of problems. After she got some help, she told me never to start drinking. Right then, I knew I didn't want to end up like her in some drug rehab.

TA.Host:	*Did anyone else have a role model that told them not to drink?*
Carlos19:	A Teen Advisor panel came to my classroom when I was in junior high to talk about drinking. I'll never forget this big senior announcing that he'd made a stand. He said he didn't have to do any ungodly things to be cool. As an athlete, he reminded us that drinking could hurt him. That impressed me a lot. Hey, I hear my dad calling. TTFN.
KitKat:	If you hang in there and stay strong, people will respect you. I remember talking on the phone with a friend who told me that she and all her friends were going out to get high, which didn't surprise me. That was a typical weekend for her. But then she said to me, "I don't feel like I should be doing that. Could I hang out with you this weekend?" She said if she was with me she wouldn't feel pressured to drink. Her phone call told me that I was making a difference. That made it all worthwhile.
MarGee:	Now THAT is very cool! :-)
LilAmy:	On the senior cruise, this one guy tried to get me to take a drink. I told him, "If I take one sip, you'll lose all respect for me. Everything I stand for would go down the drain. You wouldn't want that to happen, would you?"
Adrienne3:	What did he say?
LilAmy:	He mumbled, "No, I guess I wouldn't." See? You can take a stand! Well, it's been nice talking to you. Ciao!
Adrienne3:	Bye!

| MarGee: | TTFN! |
| KitKat: | Be strong! Stay cool! See ya! |

| TA.Host: | *Maybe you or someone you know has already tried drinking. If you or a friend have been thinking about trying "something stronger," keep reading ... I pray the next Chat Room will give you both the courage to JUST SAY NO!* |

six

Let's Chat: Why Should You "Just Say No"?

TA.Host:	*We've done a chapter on drinking, but there are other temptations we need to talk about, like smoking and doing drugs. Who wants to start?*
Nick22:	I will. I've never really been tempted to use drugs or drink beer. We learned in elementary school about the harmful effects of drugs and alcohol. But when I got to high school, it seemed like all my old friends—the ones I had grown up with—started experimenting. I found myself at a fork in the road.
Jimbo8:	Fork? What fork?
Nick22:	Well, that decision cost me most of my old friends. In fact, I wondered if I had made the wrong choice. Talk about peer pressure! But as time went on, I met more people who were like me.
Janey18:	Yeah, but I bet your old friends really got burned out and stopped doing so well in school …
Nick22:	Actually, do you know what was hardest to deal with? My friends who were drinking and smoking were still doing great in sports. These guys

showed no side effects of drug use. Then it seemed like everyone in my classes talked about partying, what they did last weekend, and what they drank or smoked. I felt as if I was missing out on an important part of high school.

NickAtNite: C'mon. You mean you NEVER even tried a drink? That's hard to believe!

Nick22: I almost did, once. Around Christmas I told one of my friends—who wasn't a TA—that I wanted to try drinking. For two nights I tried to get out of the house to go drink, but little things kept coming up. Then one of my best friends told my mom that I was going out drinking, and she set me straight. I guess that was God's way of not letting me mess up.

Robbie15: There was a time when I was bad into drugs. But when I stopped, my friends saw a drastic change in my behavior for the good, and they respected me. In a good set of friends, you have loyalty and respect, and you help each other out. If you want to take a stand and not use drugs and alcohol, you'll find it a lot easier to keep that stand if you stay with a group that isn't doing that stuff.

LilAmy: That goes for smoking, too. Smoking cigarettes has become the cool thing at school. It's such a disgusting habit. Why is smoking cool again?

TA.Mike: Fads go in cycles. But I'm not sure why kids want to smoke. It deteriorates your body. Your clothes stink, and so do you. And secondhand smoke hurts others. Last but not least, smoking can be very expensive.

Janey18:	Yeah, who has $$$ to burn?!? Ha, ha.
HectorG:	When I was a sophomore and in my first year as a TA, I went to this party put on by some of my friends who weren't TAs. I must have not been thinking that night, because they talked me into smoking with them. At first I thought I was cool, but then the girl who threw the party, who knew I was a TA and a Christian, came over to me and said, "I'm disappointed to see you smoking, Hector. I would have never expected you to do that." I was crushed! I knew my witness had been destroyed with her. As for smoking cigarettes—what a stupid thing to break a contract for!
JoeBob:	Did you get kicked out of TA for breaking your contract?
HectorG:	I took myself out of TA, but I never once smoked or drank after that. I wanted to prove to myself and others that I could do it. I returned to TA my senior year and had a wonderful experience. Because of my choices, God blessed me both spiritually and academically. And I learned two important things: 1. You have to watch yourself—no one is ever too strong to mess up. And 2. Others are always watching.
TA.Host:	*Has anyone in this chat room ever chewed tobacco?*
ReginaC:	No, but my friend's dad has to put his thumb over his throat to answer the telephone. He got throat cancer from dipping.

BBMatt:	I have. I'm a baseball player. Hey, it's a big part of the game, putting a plug in your mouth and spitting in the outfield.
BraDy3:	On my team, chewing tobacco was always passed around the dugout. But I never tried it cuz it looked like worm dirt.
JoeBob:	Did you ever tell your teammates that?
BraDy3:	Nah … but they still made fun of me for not taking a chew. Their taunts didn't bother me. In the end, they respected my choice. Besides, I'm bigger than most of them.
Micah6-8:	I'm a small sophomore, so I'm not bigger than anybody. :-) Why is chewing tobacco not a good idea?
BBMatt:	There are all sorts of bad effects from chewing snuff. It's physically and psychologically as addicting as cigarettes, and just as harmful—if not more. A dip of snuff has roughly the same amount of nicotine and ten times the nitrosamines as one cigarette.
Micah6-8:	Nitro-what?
BBMatt:	Nitrosamines. Highly potent cancer-causing substances. Chewing tobacco in your mouth is like having an incubator for all those bad germs to grow. Watch out—you could get oral cancer. Then you'd have to get a chunk of your mouth removed to save your life. (And besides it gives you really rank breath. Girls won't kiss you.)
EErika:	Why do teens chew or smoke when it makes their breath so bad?
LouiseP:	I smoked out of curiosity in eighth and ninth grade. I had been struggling with my weight,

	and I heard smoking was a good way to depress my appetite. I also thought a cigarette in my hand made me cool. I got addicted the first time I smoked a few.
EErika:	What was so addictive about smoking? Don't you know that it's a gross habit?
LouiseP:	I liked the taste and the feeling I got when I inhaled.
EErika:	Why did you stop?
LouiseP:	When I realized how bad it hurt my parents and the people around me. And I had to quit to be a Teen Advisor. But even though I've quit, I'm tempted to smoke again when I'm around others who are lighting up.
BBMatt:	This is Matt again, the guy who chewed tobacco. For me, smoking was an entry-level thing. Then I dipped in eighth grade because I got a buzz from the nicotine. Quickly, the desire to chew became a craving.
LaurieDoll:	I've heard that people who start smoking cigarettes end up smoking pot. Is that true?
BBMatt:	Let me tell you that when I was smoking a cigarette to take the place of smoking a joint, all I was thinking about was the next chance I could smoke pot. Smoking pot gave me more of a high than smoking cigarettes. I used to drive while I was high, and I'd hide the stash so it couldn't be found. I was very nervous and paranoid.
LaurieDoll:	What made you quit?
BBMatt:	I had heard that I wouldn't quit until I hit rock bottom or wanted to quit. For me, it was see-

	ing the love in my parents' eyes and knowing it would kill them to force the issue with me. My doing drugs was tearing them up. And God was telling me to live soberly. He helped me see that it was not good to abuse the gift of life I had been given.
TyroneM:	I tried pot a few times, just to be part of the group. When the joint got passed, I took a hit.
JoeBob:	So now what would you do if someone passed you a joint?
TyroneM:	Tell them I don't want it. If they didn't respect that, I'd take off. When my best friend started smoking pot as a sophomore, it bothered me. But I figured he wouldn't be my friend if I said anything, so I kept my mouth shut. But after a while, we stopped speaking to each other.
JoeBob:	What's so great about drugs that you'd give up your friends?! That seems pretty dumb.
LilaLo:	Kids are eating them up because they want a good trip. Teenagers don't look at what it's doing TO you, it's what it's doing FOR you. The only reason I did it was because it was a way to escape reality. And that wasn't a good reason.
Ganon939:	All my friends are smoking and drinking, and I'm a ninth grader. How do I handle the situation?
BBMatt:	When I was smoking pot I offered it to buddies, and they just told me that they don't smoke. Pretty plain.
TA.Host:	*How does drug use affect you mentally?*

BBMatt:	After smoking pot awhile, I started thinking about it all the time. It's something that controls your mind, slows you down. It's affected my mind after years of use. My reflexes are slower. Concentrating is hard.
BraDy3:	Did you ever think of just quitting?
BBMatt:	Sure. Even when I was smoking pot, I had a deep conviction to not do it again. I guess that the Lord was tugging at my conscience. I promised God that I would do better the next day, but then I kept doing drugs. It wasn't until I reached bottom, like I said, and asked the Lord for forgiveness and a new start that I was able to turn the corner on drugs.
meredithc:	What stopped me from doing drugs was seeing the effect that alcohol and drugs had on my friends' lives. I have one friend who has a terrible relationship with her parents. She's been kicked out of the house, and her grades are way down. She gave in to the addiction and its effects. Her drug use is hurting a lot of people's lives, and she doesn't realize it.
TA.Mike:	Have you tried to talk to her?
meredithc:	One time, I told her I was thinking about not becoming a Teen Advisor. When she learned that news, she got really mad because she thought I wanted to start hanging out with her and her friends, and she didn't want me to take up the druggie life at all.
TA.Host:	*Is there anyone else who has taken drugs who has a story to tell?*

BigBen6: I've broken my contract numerous times, and I've been before the Teen Advisor Honor Council twice. In the beginning of my junior year, I started hanging around a lot of the wrong people. They smoked a lot of pot and drank all the time. At first it was easy for me to "say no," but after a while, I saw how much fun they were having, so I tried it a few times. But I started feeling guilty, and every time I saw my parents, all I could think about was how much I was lying to them.

JoeBob: How did you get caught? Or did you turn yourself in?

BigBen6: I didn't feel bad about what I was doing, at least for a while. But thanks to God's persistence, I realized that what I was doing was wrong, and I needed to repent and turn myself in to the Teen Advisor Honor Council. But before I turned myself in, a very good friend— to this day I don't know who—told them. I'm actually thankful this person did, because now I'm doing great.

TA.Host: *We have time for one more story.*

CourtnE: I've watched the lives of several of my friends slowly slip away due to involvement with drugs, alcohol, and tobacco. We all started out as Teen Advisors together, but as we began to grow older, we split and went our different ways.

JoeBob: You mean there are TAs who get involved in DRUGS? : 0 [

CourtnE:	The contract isn't magic, JoeBob. It's all in the commitment you make. My friends' involvement with drugs was progressive. It started out with a few sips of beer here, a couple of cigarettes there. Before they knew it, they were hooked. :0[
meredithc:	How did you find out, CourtnE?
CourtnE:	One day, I was sitting at a lunch table with some of my friends. The conversation somehow got into what drugs they had done and what they were planning to do with drugs. The people at that table knew what I stood for, but they didn't care. I hurt for them and the fact that their lives were being destroyed by drugs and alcohol. While sitting at the table, my eyes began to tear up. I just couldn't handle it.
EErika:	You really started to cry in front of your classmates?
CourtnE:	Nobody saw I was upset because I had left the lunch table and gone to the bathroom. There, all alone, I cried very, very hard. After I finished, I went back to the table, cool and composed. None of my friends even knew that God had placed a burden on my heart for them. I haven't forgotten the impact of that experience. I still pray for many of my friends who are involved with drugs.
JoeBob:	Why? What difference does it make? It's their choice!
CourtnE:	I love them just the same. Perhaps I love them more because I know they are hurting. People who do drugs and alcohol often rationalize

their behavior by saying, "What I'm doing is not hurting anyone else." They just don't know how much pain they bring to others.

TA.Host: *Maybe you've lost some of your friends because of their choices ... or your own choices. Or maybe you're just feeling alone. Join us in the next Chat Room and find out what people your age do to make new friends!*

seven

Let's Chat: How Do You Make Friends?

TA.Host:	*Making new friends can be hard. How can you make it easier? Does anyone have ideas they'd like to share?*
RomonaC:	Our family is going to be moving next summer to a new state, and I'm dreading making new friends.
GinaGina:	Think of your move as a chance to start over. :-) Just be yourself. So many people try to be someone else.
GB789:	Come on, it takes more than that to make new friends.
GinaGina:	Not really. You can define "being yourself" by who you want to be and not who other people want you to be. Don't do things just because somebody in your group would want you to act that way.
Ashley99:	Sounds good, but people don't always like you just because you are your own person. Like what happened to me—people made fun of me because I was good at school.
GinaGina:	If some people end up not liking you, that's all right. No one, not even Jesus, was liked by everyone.

Ashley99:	I guess so ... I did make friends eventually.
GinaGina:	Sure! Just don't hang back and avoid people, waiting for them to come to you. Sometimes you have to initiate a conversation.
LeahLilly:	You're right! :-) That absolutely happened to me when I moved. I reached out, and people came around!
MeganT:	Me, too. Nobody from my middle school followed me to my new high school, so in ninth grade, I had to start all over again. It was hard, but by the end of my freshman year, I had friends.
MaryBeth5:	What did you do to make friends?
MeganT:	I got involved in school activities, talked to my classmates, and reached out. Sitting by myself at lunch only made me miserable :0(so I made an effort to introduce myself. That's the only reason I made any friends.
GB789:	Should I generally hang out only with Christians?
HollyBear:	That's a hard question. On one level, I think it's very important that your most intimate friends be Christians. That way you'll have two or three people who will support you in making right decisions.
HeidiLou:	You go, girl!
TA.Jen:	It will help you stay strong. I know.
HollyBear:	I learned this lesson the hard way. I hung out with a wild crowd my freshman year of high school, going to all their parties. I figured many things I did weren't so bad because all

	my friends were doing them. That wasn't good.
GB789:	So you're saying that I shouldn't hang out with non-Christian friends.
HollyBear:	I think you can hang out with non-Christians as long as you're selective. You can have a bunch of Christians and a couple non-Christian friends. Remember, we need to be a witness to others.
TA.Host:	*Besides being Christian, what other qualities should you look for in a friend?*
RossTee:	There are so many cliques in school—druggies, preps, jocks, skateboarders, brains, cheerleaders. People will naturally hang out with people they have something in common with. But don't forget that a dopehead will want to hang out with someone who smokes pot. Bad company wants to be with bad company.
TA.Jen:	Make yourself available to non-Christians. I have great friends now who were not Christians when I met them. Through our friendship and my ability to love them where they were, they were willing to listen to me.
MaryBeth5:	What do you do when a friend moves away?
BranDee:	When I got into high school, all my friends had moved away during that summer. :-(I went to the first day of classes not knowing if anyone would even care if I was there. I tried to be as friendly as I could, but it took a while to get close to anyone. I mean, what if I screwed up

and said something stupid? I felt lonely, but I tried not to show it.

Caleb42: I think it's a big mistake to hang around anyone who isn't a Christian. Non-Christians just don't have the same values!

TA.Jen: Think about a football team. They need the camaraderie in the locker room to make the team work. But what if they stayed in the locker room and never played the game? What's the point? I think that's a lesson we can learn as Christians as far as relationships are concerned. Yeah, we can sit around and encourage each other all day long, but God has called us to get out there and love others.

TA.Host: *What if your parents don't approve of your friends?*

TA.Jen: Try to find out why, calmly and respectfully. They may have good reasons. Ask if you can have certain friends over at your house, so your parents can get to know them better. Once they get to know your friends, they may feel more comfortable with them.

HeidiLou: My mom is always thrilled when I invite kids over for dinner. She loves to cook!

MaryBeth5: Yeah, but if your parents still bug you about certain friends, it's probably easier if you just make some other friends. You don't have to be a snob—you can still be friendly at school. But it's important to listen to your parents.

AAAGuy: My parents don't like skateboarders and guys

	who sag, but they are cool guys. Why can't I hang out with them?
Rusty2000:	There's certainly nothing wrong with someone who rides a skateboard, but what those guys are doing when they're not skateboarding may compromise some things for you.
AAAGuy:	LOL No way. Like what?
Rusty2000:	Well, do they smoke? Party? Lie? Have bad reps with girls? Solid friendships are based on loyalty, trust, honesty, and respect. You should spend time with people who respect your values.
RossTee:	I've never been part of the cool crowd, but I've heard that to be part of that crowd you have to change yourself. These days, I have one best friend. Instead of being cool with each other, we respect our differences. You can't have differences within the cool crowd.
TomTunes:	The question I hate most on panels is "How do I make friends?" There's no easy formula. It's up to you—deciding what you want to be and who will be your friends. I once dated a Teen Advisor who broke her contract and wouldn't own up to it. When I asked her about it, she called me names and said I was chicken not to drink.
AAAGuy:	>8-0 Wow! That would really make me mad!
TomTunes:	Yeah, I really considered falling for her lines. I almost gave in and drank with her. That afternoon, my mom confronted me in her loving way because my best friend had informed on

	me. When I talked to him later about it and asked him why, he said that he did it because I had too much going for me. He really proved what kind of friend he was.
NickAtNite:	Yeah. A snitch.
TomTunes:	No. A real friend.
AAAGuy:	I'm going to change the subject here. What if all my friends want to go see a real popular NC-17 movie?
BrittanE:	It's going to be tough saying you're not going to go. Start looking for friends who don't go to NC-17 flicks. In other words, look for others with the same morals as you.
GB789:	Any other advice you can give me on hanging out with the right crowd?
Rusty2000:	You may have to look around, but there are people just like you waiting to become your friend. Just get out there and make something happen. Be proactive, not reactive.
TA.ML:	Be careful about the friends you choose. Keep an open line of communication with your parents or adults you trust and can confide in, such as your youth group leader. If you are feeling pressured or afraid in school, tell your parents or your youth leader about it. Remember: pick friends you respect, not because they're doing the cool things, but because you think they're honest.
Agriffin:	What will happen to my friends after I graduate from high school?
TA.Jen:	I've been lucky because most of my good high school friends are still very close to me. But

HeidiLou:	I've made some very good friends in college, and the making-friends part just boils down to being honest upfront about who you are. That doesn't always happen, though. Just try to appreciate your friends for the time you have them. Sometimes God gives us friends for a time ... and sometimes, friends forever.
TA.Host:	*Whether you have a friend for a short time or for the rest of your life, it takes two to make it work. Dating is like that, too. Stay with us and hear what others are saying about the guy-girl thing!*

eight

Let's Chat: About the Guy-Girl Thing

TA.Host:	*Should you or shouldn't you? Whom should you go with and how often should you go out? Alone or in groups? Dating is a huge topic for teens. Who wants to start?*
MeghanM:	During my first two years of high school, I never dated. Dating wasn't really important to me. None of my friends had serious boyfriends.
HeidiLou:	I didn't date until I was a junior. My mother wouldn't let me.
BANDIT16:	I first went out with a girl when I was thirteen. To the movies. (My mother drove—not too embarrassing.)
MeghanM:	Even though I didn't date right away, my mother taught me a lot about the rights and wrongs of being a girl. "Don't chase after boys, they'll just run faster," she said. "Don't call boys, let them call you."
Carlos19:	You're kidding! Girls call me all the time! And I LOVE it!
Dan0831:	Not me. I would rather call a girl myself. Your mother is right on, Meghan.
JoeFtball:	Should a girl ever call a guy for a date?

Tamika:	I don't think girls should just ask guys out. But if you're just good friends and you both would like to go out, it's OK to call and ask what he's doing on the weekend. You don't have to give a big explanation. Just be casual.
Bridget17:	My parents have told me to let the guy do the pursuing. I can call guy friends. But for dating, they say he should call me.
Micah6-8:	I think Bridget is right. I went on a date with this girl once, and she called me every night for the next week. I got tired of her calls and lost interest. It was like I was being persuaded to be her boyfriend. I didn't like it.
BigBen6:	I agree. I've been asked out by girls before, and I would rather ask the girl out.
TrishA!:	My mother told me not to call boys. "His mother will get tired of you calling," she told me.
Carlos19:	I still think it's OK if a girl asks me out. It can relieve a lot of stress if that happens.
JoeFtball:	Have you been asked out by a girl?
Carlos19:	Sort of. I have been pursued.
JoeFtball:	Did you like it?
Carlos19:	I don't know. It was OK.
JoeFtball:	Come on, give us a straight answer here.
Carlos19:	Well….
TA.Host:	*Let's change the subject a bit. How involved are your parents in your dating relationships?*
MeghanM:	Parents should definitely have a big say-so in their children's decisions on dating. Otherwise, you might end up with the wrong guy.

TA.Anne: My parents set certain rules about dating. I couldn't car date until I was sixteen. I could only have dates in the house when my parents were home, but we couldn't go in the bedroom. And my mom used to tell me, "Don't get too comfortable with your date!" If we were in the kitchen, my parents would walk in constantly. Also, I could only see my boyfriend two nights a week, but that did not include church activities.

Tina@12: Your parents were strict! How did you put up with them?

TA.Anne: Yes, they were pretty strict. But they were also consistent and firm—and they love me a lot!

HeidiLou: If a guy doesn't want to go by my parents' rules, he's not worth dating. And if he doesn't even want to meet my parents—forget it!

Jenna16: My dates have to meet my big brother. He's a lot scarier than my father.

TA.Host: *I've heard that some high schoolers put off dating one-on-one, and spend most of the time having "group dates." Have any of you heard of that?*

TA.Missy: Group dating in high school is one of the healthiest things you can do. So many times, kids in high school who get involved in dating relationships end up having a mini-divorce. They're devastated. Teenagers are not emotionally, financially, or spiritually ready to be married. Yet, some of them are in relationships that are like a little marriage.

Tim888-4: How big should a group be?

TA.Missy:	Six to ten people. It doesn't have to be an even number of girls and guys. Group dating will help you develop friendships with the opposite sex in a godly, healthy way with no ulterior motives.
Janette:	What's "ulterior motives"? You mean sex?
TA.Missy:	Not always. For girls especially it's just as important to guard your hearts. Girls are notorious for just saying too much to a guy. Once you've shared your heart to a guy, you become emotionally bonded to him, whether you mean to or not.
ValerieV:	My older sister says dating is a lot of fun. I'm a sophomore, and I want to start dating too!
Rusty2000:	Dating is fun, sure. But along with dating comes responsibility. Do you think you're prepared to take on the responsibility that comes with dating?
ValerieV:	Well, I don't know. What kind of responsibility are you talking about?
Rusty2000:	When you start dating someone, especially if you're a guy, you have a responsibility not just for yourself, but also for the person you're dating.
ValerieV:	But my interest is in having a good time.
Rusty2000:	You can have a great time with people without having a dating relationship. A lot of times when you're dating someone, you miss out on a lot of great friendships because you're focused on one individual.
ValerieV:	So if I go out with a lot of other people, I'll make more friends than pairing off one-on-one?

Rusty2000: Absolutely. That's certainly not to say that dating is inherently wrong. But there are a lot of potential pitfalls that go along with dating if it's not thought through. That's why I prefer group dating.

ValerieV: If I take your advice and go for this group dating thing, what are some fun things to do? I don't want to go miniature golfing all the time.

Rusty2000: That's a great question. Some of the great group dates I've had are cooking dinner with a bunch of friends. We would go to the grocery store together, buy food, and go back to one of our parents' homes to start cooking. One time after making chicken fajitas, we sat around and played cards. That was one of the best group dates I've ever had. There was no pressure.

ValerieV: Were there any boyfriend/girlfriends at this dinner thing?

Rusty2000: No, it was just friends hanging out, and that's the way it should be in high school. You should be getting totally comfortable going out with a group of friends, guys and girls, without worrying what the other sex will think.

DanBoy: I'm an eighth grader. Are you saying that I really shouldn't date until high school?

Rusty2000: My personal opinion is that you're better off doing the group dating thing. It's just a healthier way to go. Just get a group of friends and go out and have a good time.

ValerieV: Did you date in high school?

Rusty2000: I only had one steady relationship, the rest of my time I went on group dates. Looking back,

	I would have been just as happy sticking with the group dating scene.
Erik203:	About group dating, we would go bowling or just get together and watch a movie at my house. Some people think that's only for junior high kids, but it's not.
TA.Host:	*Are there any bad sides to dating one-on-one?*
HeidiLou:	There are good and bad sides to everything. I'm not dating anyone now, but I'm having fun with my friends.
MeghanM:	Heidi's right. Having a boyfriend can put a damper on friendships with others. I'm glad I didn't start dating until a little later in my high school career. I think it's better to be single for a while. You have the rest of your life to be with just one person when you reach the marrying age. Now you can just hang out with your friends.
Ashley99:	I dated a guy for a couple of months during my junior year. I came out of the relationship realizing that life is sometimes better when you're not dating. He wanted all my attention, so I didn't have any other friends. We broke up, and I had a blast my senior year because I had more free time. I could focus on all my friends instead of just one person.
LaurieDoll:	Yeah, I've really struggled with balancing my time between my friends and my boyfriend. Experience has taught me not to tune out my friends when I have a steady boyfriend. It can be tough, however.

TA.Host:	*What would you say is the most important quality in the person you date?*
BigBen6:	Beautiful eyes. LOL
ValerieV:	Knows how to have fun!
Jenna16:	Honesty, definitely. And caring.
Martha14:	If you're a Christian, you can only date other Christians. Scripture is very clear.
Ashley99:	Yeah. "Don't be unequally yoked with unbelievers."
HeidiLou:	"A threefold cord is not easily broken." My mother says the three folds are you, the other person—and God.
Rusty2000:	Scripture also says there's no fellowship with darkness. I went out with a young lady not long ago, and one of the first things we talked about was our relationship with Christ.
JulieK:	I'm with Rusty. Couples who are "unequally yoked" will bring each other down. If my relationships do not honor the Lord, then I would rather not date.
HollyBear:	I'm picky about guys. I won't go out with a guy unless he's a Christian and doesn't drink or do drugs.
SuzieQ:	Really? Did you ever tell a guy to hit the road?
HollyBear:	In so many words, yes. There was one guy my freshman year. He knew what I was like, but he lied to me to get a date. When I learned that, I broke it off.
TA.Host:	*Has anyone here dated a non-Christian, hoping to bring him or her to the Lord?*
PhaedraD:	The very first time I ever dated was when I was

fifteen. I thought I was mature enough to handle anything that came my way. Well, the first guy I dated was not a Christian. (He said he was, but I later learned he wasn't.) I told myself that it was OK since I could draw him closer to the Lord.

HollyBear: Big mistake. What happened?

PhaedraD: For almost ten months we dated, and I got my heart really involved. I never did compromise myself physically—we never did anything but kiss—but my spiritual life suffered. You see, I had transferred my trust and faith in God to this guy.

JulieK: When you realized this, did you break up with him?

PhaedraD: Not right away. But that summer I realized that I needed God as my first love. I didn't know what to do even though I had been praying about it so much. Well, the guy broke up with me on the first day of school—which was a break for me. After our breakup, I knew that my life was now in the Lord's hands, and He awesomely healed my heart. It was then that I made a written commitment to God, stating that I wasn't going to have a boyfriend in high school. I would focus on Him and dispense with the dating scene in high school.

SherryV: I've been dating a lot, and there's no way I'm going to go through high school without dating guys. Are there any TAs out there who can relate to me?

MiMichelle: Throughout middle school and high school, there have only been a few times when I have not had a boyfriend. Almost every one of these relationships has grown out of friendship. Perhaps that's because I have always strongly believed in dating someone who shares my values, and that is something I highly recommend for you.

SherryV: Why? There's nothing wrong with just going out.

SooSandra: I think it's better to wait and find the right person, but I'll grant you that's easier said than done.

Lindsey04: My mom advised me to be picky. Don't compromise your standards.

Ashley99: I've always been tall and skinny, and I'm a model. I know now that guys will like me for who I am. But you know something? My standards are too high for most of them. One guy broke up with me, saying I was the kind of a girl he wanted to marry, but not the kind he wanted to date.

RockinTina: What did he mean by that?

Ashley99: I think he was looking for someone to sleep with.

MiMichelle: Whatever person you choose to have a relationship with must share your beliefs and values, and you should choose a boyfriend who will enhance your relationship with God.

SherryV: But it's hard to find someone who shares your values! Haven't you ever been alone on a Saturday night?

MiMichelle: Of course. But even though I've had many boyfriends, I honestly believe that I could be just as happy without one. Many of my friends do not have boyfriends, and they are some of the happiest people I know. The bottom line is that you do not have to have a girlfriend or boyfriend to make your life complete.

TA.Host: *What do you find most challenging about the dating scene?*

JJHurt: I'm a guy, and I have a real hard time talking to girls. I get these sweaty palms and worry that I'm going to say something stupid. What can I do?

BikeNJoel: If you're trying to talk to a girl, don't think of that person as being the opposite sex. Think of that person as your friend. She is just like you in many ways. We all laugh, cry, and care about the same things. It took me a while to realize this. I used to have problems talking to girls. But it's not so hard. You just have to try it out a few times.

JJHurt: Are you dating anyone now, Joel? Or is this theory?

BikeNJoel: I've been dating someone for about six months, and she has become a best friend to me. We can talk about anything, and we know we can trust the other person to listen and care about what we say. But in order to get this way, we had to start talking. When we first met, I often felt nervous just starting a conversation with her. I know it's hard, but believe me, you can do it! If you don't, you will always wonder what might have been if you could have just gotten up the courage to talk to him or her. It's really not that hard. Like the Nike ad says: Just do it!

TA.Host: *OK, everyone. Time for our next topic. When it comes to dating, how far is too far?*

nine

Let's Chat: How Far Is Too Far?

TA.Host:	*So, how far is too far? Who wants to start?*
NickAtNite:	My parents said that since I'm a mature sixteen-year-old, I can start dating. What can I do to get in with the ladies?
Bruce24:	One thing guys can do for their dates is not put any sexual pressure on them.
Jenna16:	I'll say! It's a relief not to have to defend myself at the end of a date.
NickAtNite:	OK, I'm not going to make any inappropriate moves on my girlfriend. But what about a goodnight kiss?
CourtnE:	That's a big worry for girls—and guys. There's no rule that says you have to kiss after the first date, and I have friends who dated for *months* before kissing.
BMOC:	Is it OK to French kiss?
Rusty2000:	Here's the issue: What will French kissing lead to? I've French-kissed before, and there were times where it led to more stuff. I regret that. A good rule of thumb: If what you are doing makes you want to do more, stop doing it, even if it's just holding hands or hugging closely.

TA.Jen: I would say don't even be in a hurry to hold hands. Believe it or not, girls worry about that. It's a great relief to a girl when a guy just treats her like a sister.

JohnJr: If I can jump in here, my girlfriend and I knew we wouldn't have sex in the dating relationship. We even discussed it before we ever went out. I wanted to be her boyfriend because I knew what she stood for. That's what attracted me to her.

TA.Host: *How important is it to set limits BEFORE you start dating?*

BrittanE: VERY important. It's especially important to be clear on what you expect early in the relationship, so there are no misunderstandings.

Catherine14: The more physical you are with a guy, the less he'll respect you. If you tell the guy that right from the beginning and he agrees to it, he won't be expecting anything more.

ReginaC: That's true, provided BOTH members of the couple truthfully agree on their limits. Otherwise they will be on different wavelengths. And if your boyfriend or girlfriend think its time to *change* those limits, then it's time to *talk again*.

Robbie15: My girlfriend and I decided on the "bathing suit" rule. We agreed we wouldn't touch any part of the body covered by a bathing suit.

NickAtNite: Is that bikini or wet suit? LOL

Robbie15: OK, smart guy. From the neck to the knees is off limits? Got it?

NickAtNite: SOME bathing suit! :-)

Davidson2: What happens if you kinda go beyond your limits?

BrookeT: When Joel and I first started dating, we struggled with the gray areas between kissing and having sex. When we went past our limits, we regrouped and asked for God's forgiveness.

Valerie20: Unfortunately, my boyfriend and I passed all the limits, and we, too, prayed and asked for forgiveness. I should have seen it coming, however. My boyfriend's sister told me not to trust Josh to be responsible for my limits, so I have to take some of the blame.

TA.Host: *Asking for God's forgiveness and taking steps to help you resist temptation in the future are both important if you're serious about abstaining from sexual sin. How have you found it helpful to avoid repeating the same mistakes over and over?*

Danielle3: Whether you're trying to keep pure, or trying to get back on track after messing up (some call it "second virginity"), you need to be careful. Here are some pointers I use in my own life:

1. Make sure that when you go out you know what you'll be doing for the night. You should have plans for the whole evening. In other words, if you're going out to a 7:00 movie but don't have to be home until 11:30, you better have plans for the other two-and-a-half hours. Movies aren't four hours long last time I checked. Idle time for us teenagers can definitely be trouble.

2. Don't have a ten-minute good-bye kiss. We all know a lot can happen in a short amount of time. Long kissing can lead to heavy petting.

3. Watch how much time you're spending alone with your date. It could be too much time playing with temptation. Don't set yourself up for a fall.

4. It's OK for your parents to forbid you from seeing someone they don't feel is right. My own parents have had to do this with me in the past. I look back and see how right they were.

5. Don't be afraid of strict rules. Your parents are doing you a favor by laying out a list of rules. Even if they hassle you, someday you will thank them.

HeidiLou: I've heard of a program called "True Love Waits." Anyone here know about that?

BigBrian: I heard about the "True Love Waits" program in my church youth group, and I like what I heard. My junior year I made a solemn vow before God about what my standards should be. I vowed to God, my parents, my future wife, and my future children that I would remain sexually pure until the day I marry.

LaurieDoll: How cool! :-)

Valerie20: Looking back, I probably should have made a pact like that before I started dating. There's only so much physical stuff two people can do. After that, there's nothing left. Then you wish holding hands was enough. One thing I'm try-

	ing to learn is to be in love with the Lord before being in love with anybody.
Jinny14:	Right. If you decide not to kiss every time you see each other, it makes the times you do kiss very special.
TA.Anne:	My father did something I will cherish the rest of my life. On my thirteenth birthday, my father took me on my first date. He told me how special I was and how important it was to stay physically pure until I got married. Dad then handed me a beautiful gold necklace with a heart and a key on it, saying that it represented the key to my heart and my body. I was to wear it as a reminder of how important it was to keep myself pure for my future husband.
Valerie20:	That's nice ... but did it work?
TA.Anne:	Oh, yes. The importance of that night became even greater when I gave my husband the key to my heart on my wedding night. The key has been soldered into his wedding band.
TA.Host:	*When you talk about "going too far," most people think we're talking about sexual intimacy. But are there other dating mistakes couples make, besides sexual ones?*
Rusty2000:	There is one important one I can think of. It has to do with guarding your heart, like we talked about earlier. Saying the words "I love you" is a dangerous thing. Those are words that are tossed around far too much today. I've had girls tell me, "You know, I struggle when a guy tells me that he loves me."

KissMeKate: Why is that? Don't we all want to be loved?

Rusty2000: When a girl hears "I love you," it affects her emotions. It's different for guys, who are often more casual about it. That's one of the things that they taught me.

KissMeKate: I wouldn't have guessed that. I just thought you were supposed to tell your boyfriend "I love you" after you've gone out a bunch of times.

Rusty2000: It's one of those areas of responsibility, like I talked about before. Saying "I love you" is one of those things that you should not say if you're not mature enough to think about marriage. But don't worry about it. You'll get there. Just cool your jets until then.

TA.Host: *Has anyone run into unusual dating situations, where you didn't know what was the right thing to do?*

Ganon939: Not yet, but I'm going to the senior prom. What is acceptable behavior on my part?

Rusty2000: If you're talking about physical intimacy, I think the question is not "How close can I get?" or "How far can I go?" but *"How far away should I stay?"* When in doubt, the smart thing is to keep your distance, if you know what I mean.

Lostinlove: I'm dating an older guy. What will happen if he goes off to college?

Polli2: I dated a senior when I was just a freshman. We got involved almost accidentally, and before things got too hot, we agreed not to let the

	relationship get too serious because he was going to college.
Lostinlove:	So, did everything work out? I really like this guy.
Polli2:	Sorry. It was not a healthy relationship because I was much younger than him. He never called me unless he had nothing else to do on a Friday night, so I always had to stick close to the phone in case he called. He lied to me about where he was going and who he would be with. And he often broke dates. When he did show up, all he wanted to do was make out!
Lostinlove:	That's pretty bad.
Polli2:	It got worse. One time he grabbed my arm so hard that he bruised me, and several times he pushed me around or slapped me!
Lostinlove:	How come you didn't dump this guy? He sounds like a loser.
Polli2:	Honestly, I don't know why I stayed with him so long. I guess I thought that if I tried hard enough, he would like me, maybe even love me. I knew that he wanted to break up with me, but he wouldn't for some reason. It hurt a lot, but I ended up breaking the relationship.
Lostinlove:	You cried over this loser?
Polli2:	When he wasn't mean, he made me feel special—I mean, a SENIOR wanted to date me! My parents were overjoyed when we broke up, even though they didn't know the whole thing. I wish they knew what really happened, but I was too afraid to tell them. I just wish

	that someone had taken the time to help me see what kind of guy he really was. I don't know, maybe I wouldn't have listened anyway. I just had to learn the hard way. I learned a good lesson, but a lot of hurt and tears would have been avoided if I'd not been so blind to the red flags early on.
CassondraT:	What if things aren't really that bad—he's not hitting me or anything. What if the relationship just isn't going where you want it to go?
TA.Anne:	If you are having a hard time communicating with your boyfriend, a good thing would be to pray together or *for* him. You will be amazed at what this will do for your relationship.
CassondraT:	I would feel awfully uncomfortable praying with my boyfriend. You don't know him.
TA.Anne:	If he's uncomfortable praying with you, then maybe you're dating the wrong person.
Tina@12:	But if she breaks up with her boyfriend, she might be alone a long time. Having a boyfriend or girlfriend is a big part of being in high school!
TA.Anne:	Based on my experiences in high school, I don't think that's true. I spent my freshman and half of my sophomore year not really dating seriously. Sure, I felt out of it when I saw my friends dating, and there were times I felt miserable. But when I got tired of being so miserable, I decided to date Christ.
Tina@12:	Wait a minute. Did you say that you started dating Christ?
TA.Anne:	Yes, I did. In other words, I decided I was

going to focus on my relationship with the Lord. And because I was faithful in my relationship with Christ, He brought a wonderful man into my life totally unexpectedly. This man became my boyfriend for the next five years and is now my husband.

Tina@12: That's a nice fairy tale ending, but if I heard you right, you also said you were miserable.

TA.Anne: I was miserable when I was in high school. But I often tell my friends who are not dating that they should learn to focus on Christ and what He has in store for them. If you are faithful, He will bless you unexpectedly. Dating is not all it's cracked up to be. There is a lot of junk that comes with dating someone, like arguments and just the stress of trying to relate to someone. Be content with where you are.

TA.Host: *Still not convinced that waiting to have sex is the best thing for you? Stay with us 'cause Teen Advisors are really big on this subject. Let's see what's cookin' in the next Chat Room.*

ten

Let's Chat: Why Wait?

TA.Host:	*Sex is a big subject for many teens ... and many of you must have some strong opinions about the subject. Anyone have a story to get us started?*
Danielle3:	I know a girl who was raised in a Christian family, went to a wonderful Christian school, had good friends, and had a sheltered life. She met a guy when she was seventeen, and they started dating. A few months into the relationship, she had sex with him. Nobody knew, but a few months passed, and then everyone knew. She was pregnant, and she's eighteen now with a five-month old little boy. This girl is my sister.
Rusty2000:	It's sad, but that happens a lot these days. Even among Christians. What happened to her?
Danielle3:	Fortunately, my sister made the best of a bad situation. Her boyfriend married her, and they're raising their little boy with the Lord. However, most situations don't turn out this way.
PhoeBD:	Why didn't your sister or her boyfriend use birth control?
TA.Jen:	It doesn't matter. The only sure form of birth

	control is *self*-control! That means saving sex for marriage!
SophSam:	If that's true, why do schools pass out condoms and teach us about safe sex?
Rusty2000:	A lot of people think that as long as you practice safe sex that it's OK. That's the biggest lie. There's no such thing as "safe sex." Safe sex does not exist outside of marriage. There's some dramatic figures for sexually transmitted diseases in the last decade, and the last I checked, over twenty of those diseases didn't even have a cure. That's frightening.
TA.Host:	*Let's talk more about what you hear in school. Are they telling you all you need to know?*
Adrienne3:	I don't think so. They say that all it takes to keep down teen pregnancy and sexually transmitted diseases is "education." But when sex is taught in public school health classes, there are no personal experiences shared, no tears, no mistakes. All we hear are just the facts—facts about boy parts, girl parts, and if you really want to be safe, you'll use some sort of protection.
Cris99:	Yeah, sex is everywhere: It's on TV, in the movies, sung in music, plastered all over magazines. It's no wonder why so many teenagers are having sex at younger ages every year.
JamNJeff:	Staying sexually pure is definitely a hard thing to do in today's world. There are a lot of things that push kids to have sex—and not enough to push against it. When schools pass

	out condoms, they're sending the wrong message. When soap operas and movies show everyone jumping into bed, they're sending the wrong message.
GordieMcD:	But it doesn't really matter anyway. Teens are going to have sex, no matter what anyone else tells us. We hear that in school all the time.
TA.Jen:	I've heard that argument. *You know, let's just give them protection because they're going to do it anyway.* But it's not true. I'm twenty-two years old, and I haven't done it. I was cheerleading captain in high school. I went and pledged a sorority in college. I've led a happy, productive life. I've dated and had boyfriends. I've done all those things, and I haven't had sex. And I won't say it's been easy because God created sexual desire, but we have self-control and the Holy Spirit to help us. We can choose not to do it.
TA.Host:	*Why do you think so many teenagers are having sex?*
Cris99:	I have friends who've told me that they had sex with their boyfriends or girlfriends because they were afraid they'd be dumped or made fun of if they didn't. Well, as an eighteen-year-old virgin male, I'm here to say that it doesn't have to be that way. If you hear someone say, "If you love me, you'll make love to me," your response should be, "If you love me, you wouldn't pressure me to do it." Like most teenagers, I've been tempted many times to have sex, but I went against the flow. I didn't do it!

MissMindy:	One of the biggest mistakes I ever made was having sex before marriage. I was sixteen, and my boyfriend and I had been going out for about six months. He had had sex many times before. I had told him at the beginning of our relationship that I was a virgin, and I did not want to have sex before marriage.
HeidiLou:	I was in a situation like that once. It didn't last for long, though—the guy kept pressuring me until I had to give in or break up with him. Fortunately, we broke up.
MissMindy:	I wish I had. I didn't feel the pressure at the time. He would ask me if I wanted to make love every now and then, and each time I said no. But looking back I can see how his questions weighed on me. It got me thinking about sex a lot—what it would be like. One day we were making out, and then it happened—I had sex with him. I cried myself to sleep that night. We hadn't used any kind of protection, and I was scared.
Rusty2000:	Did you break up with him?
MissMindy:	No, but I made him promise we wouldn't do it again. A month later we had sex again. Over the course of the next year, we had sex several times. I was so disgusted with myself that I contemplated suicide. We never used protection, and I was constantly scared that I might be pregnant. One day after having sex, he left and I didn't hear from him for six months. Meanwhile, my relationships with my friends and family had collapsed, so I didn't have any

	outside support. When he finally did call back, I tried to do whatever it took to make us close again. I guess part of me hoped we'd get married so everything would be all right. That didn't happen.
SuzieQ:	That must have hurt a lot.
HeidiLou:	Yes, but you're probably better off now.
MissMindy:	I knew I had made a really big mistake. I tried to get my life back together. I prayed to God to forgive me for my sins, and I made some new friends. The hardest thing I did was tell Mom. I disappointed her so much. I tell Mom everything now. I have promised myself and God that I will never have sex again until I am married.
KB761:	Has your promise stuck?
MissMindy:	Yes, it has, and by doing this, I have gained secondary virginity. Although technically I cannot be a virgin again, God's forgiveness and His grace have washed me clean. Still, it's been hard for me to forget. I should have listened to my parents. They never liked my boyfriend.
Wendy26:	Yes, but there are some things you have to learn for yourself. Next time you'll know.
TA.Jen:	What did you learn from this?
MissMindy:	I wish I knew then what I know now. The kind of guys I want to date don't want to date girls who aren't virgins. I'm dating this wonderful guy right now, and my parents love him to death, but I'm scared one day he'll find out that I'm not a virgin and break up with me.
HeidiLou:	Pray about it. If your relationship grows deep

	enough to consider marriage, you'll need to tell him. If he's the one God has for you, it will work out. He may not be thrilled, but he'll love you anyway. Just don't forget to guard your heart.
MissMindy:	The biggest lesson I learned was there's a big difference between what IS right and what FEELS right. If you think that if you and your boyfriend are in love that it's OK to have sex, you're wrong! It's never OK to have premarital sex. Girls, be strong and say no.
CassondraT:	But what does it matter if I wait? I'm planning to marry my boyfriend.
TA.Anne:	If you think it doesn't matter, you're wrong. Waiting will make your wedding night a wonderful and guilt-free experience. I know; I've been there.
mr.mike:	Of course, it's not just the girl's job to draw the line. It always takes two to tango. But even when you're considering marriage, it's important to be careful. Even more important, in fact. The last thing you want is to misuse God's most precious gift to you.
Tina@12:	But what happens if you are tempted to go too far physically?
TA.Anne:	If that happens, think about your wedding night. What do you want that evening to be like? Do you want it to be one of those once-in-a-lifetime experiences? Or just another night?
TA.Host:	*What are some of the other dangers of premarital sex?*

TA.Jen: Abortion, for one. I'm adamantly pro-life and very outspoken, and one time I was with a girlfriend. We were having a lively conversation about someone who had an abortion. I commented, "I don't see how anyone could have an abortion and kill their little baby." My friend broke down and admitted to me that she'd had an abortion at sixteen, and no one knew except the father of the child and now me.

JeterMan: Do you keep in contact with your friend who had an abortion?

TA.Jen: I sure do. And you know what she has said to me? "You're so lucky you're a virgin. I wish somebody had told me that once you give up your virginity, it's gone."

RobertL8: That sounds like the story singer Amy Grant likes to tell. When she was in her early twenties, some girls who weren't virgins were giving her a hard time. And you know what her response was? "I can be like you anytime I want," said Amy. "But you can never again be like me."

GinaGina: Does it get easier to stay pure? When has it been the most difficult for you? Is it when you're starting to get interested in the opposite sex, like from sixteen to nineteen?

TA.Jen: Actually, I think staying pure is getting harder for me now than when I was in high school. I don't know whether it's because I'm getting older or whether I'm getting deeper into relationships. What helps is that I know who I am better.

77Sunset:	What are you doing to make sure you remain pure?
TA.Jen:	I've learned through Teen Advisors that it's best to get to know each other and become friends before you get into a physical relationship. You know, I had a wonderful relationship with a guy in high school. We dated for a year and a half, and all we did was kiss. It wasn't a weird relationship. It was a normal high school relationship where we developed a friendship and respect for one another. We talked about our physical relationship from the very beginning.
77Sunset:	Really? What did you two say?
TA.Jen:	Before I dated him, I told him I had gone further than kissing. Nothing extreme, but I had engaged in some petting. Then I went to a Bible study called "Picking and Choosing a Winner," which was about choosing a mate. One of the things we were challenged to do was set up physical limits and forgive ourselves if we had gone beyond those limits at an earlier time. We also had to ask forgiveness of the people that we'd gone beyond that limit with and to commit ourselves to observing that limit from then on.
GinaGina:	Did you call up your old boyfriend? I can't imagine being able to do that.
TA.Jen:	Yes, because I took this very seriously. I called up two or three guys that I'd made out with before and apologized for any time that I ever tempted them to go further. These guys weren't

	Christians. A couple of them laughed in my face. But it was something I needed to do.
GinaGina:	If you'd gone farther than kissing before, it must have been REALLY hard not to do it later.
TA.Jen:	It was. But when I started dating Chad, my high school boyfriend, I told him on our first date that I had drawn my limit at my neck. "So, if you have any plans for dating me for any period of time, you better pace yourself," I said. A look of shock came over his face. But that was all that needed to be said.
77Sunset:	You said he was shocked. What happened next?
TA.Jen:	I don't remember. I think he said, "Great." Anyway, he respected that. What happened after that is that we went out for a month before he kissed me for the first time. Even then, we had limits for ourselves. We even had a little code word we used when we felt that we'd been kissing too much. We'd say, "Gertrude has come for a visit."
77Sunset:	Say what?
TA.Jen:	That meant we needed to stop kissing. And then we'd go do something else to take our minds off kissing. To this day, Chad and I are great friends. I think a lot of it is because there was no shame involved in our relationship at all.
TA.Host:	*Let's go back to the original question. What are reasons you have found convincing to say no to sex before marriage?*

Rusty2000: First of all, the Bible is very clear that sex is reserved for marriage only and sex was created for marriage. For those who aren't Christians, though, there are two very good arguments—the consequences of premarital sex, and our own example.

BluJean: What kind of consequences?

Rusty2000: Out-of-wedlock pregnancies and STDs, for example. Did you know that it costs nearly $500 a month to care for a little infant? That's just for basic care. Kids get more expensive as they get older. How many teenagers do you know who have that kind of money? And now there are diseases that may keep you from having children—or worse. There's HIV and AIDS. But you can also pick up less-publicized viruses that can also kill you—like HPV—that are many times more prevalent than AIDS. Do you really want to have sex that bad?

GinaGina: What did you mean about persuading kids by your example?

Rusty2000: Well, that can be very effective—although sometimes it backfires. When I was a high school senior, I remember doing a "Sex and Dating" panel for a group of sixth graders and telling them that I was a virgin. And you know what? They laughed in my face. They told me that nobody was a virgin anymore these days, and that everybody had sex. I looked at them and said, "I'm eighteen years old, and I've never had sex." And they laughed again! That floored me, to have sixth-graders laughing at

	me because they thought it was an absurd notion not to have sex!
TA.Missy:	That's very unusual. Kids seem to respond most when I say, "I'm waiting. I'm a virgin." When I was dating David, who was a high school senior, captain of the football team and real stud, he flat-out told our whole freshman class that he was a virgin and planned on staying that way. People knew that our relationship was pure.
JoeAthlete:	You mean that when an eighteen-year-old football player says, "I'm a virgin and plan to remain that way until marriage," kids really listen?
TA.Missy:	Yeah. I'm starting to see more and more the power of example. I also work full time for Teen Advisors these days, and like Rusty, I'm proud to say that I'm twenty-six years old and I can still wait to have sex. I'm thankful that on my honeymoon night I won't have to look back on my life with all these regrets. Sure, sex will be new and awkward at first, but it will be beautiful and the way God designed it to be.
Kerry909:	How important is your faith in helping you stay pure?
TA.Missy:	I honestly don't know how people without God can keep from having sex because I have to admit that it can get really hard to say no. I know it's harder for guys because men are more driven by sight. For girls, it's not as hard. For us, sex communicates a sense of commitment and security. It's like the old saying: "A

guy gives love so he'll get sex, and a girl gives sex so she'll get love."

TA.Host: *So it takes a real man to wait, right?*

TA.Missy: Yes, I do think it takes a real man to wait, to say no. Anybody can go with how he or she feels, what their bodies are telling them. But it's harder to wait. Harder, but worth it. : -)

TA.Host: *We've been talking about sexual intimacy in dating relationships here. But many teens, especially guys, experience sexual temptation in the area of pornography. If you or someone you know struggles in this area, keep reading....*

eleven

Guy's Chat: Secret Struggles With Pornography

TA.Host:	*We have with us a Teen Advisor who wants to help others by talking about his own addiction to porn. Drew, how did you first get into it?*
Drew24:	From my father. I found dirty magazines in the house when I was in fourth grade. Then we had HBO and Showtime cable channels, and when my parents weren't around, I'd watch some pretty racy stuff. I got addicted to looking at naked women.
Jimbo8:	Did your parents find out?
Drew24:	My dad tried to talk to me about it, but that didn't help me much. It wasn't until I became a Christian that I started to deal with pornography in my life.
Jer-Jer:	What's the big deal about looking at a few pictures?
Drew24:	Porn really destroys your mind. Several years after watching those movies or looking through those magazines, I can have flashbacks. It's like these images of naked women come back into my brain, and I am powerless to stop it. Porn really plays with your mind. It's like a perma-

	nent imprint. It's powerful stuff, which means that you should *flee* from it.
TTI:	How have you dealt with the flashbacks?
Drew24:	Not very well, so I've made myself accountable to a couple of buddies. They will ask me pertinent questions like: "Are you watching R-rated movies again?" "Did you struggle last week?" "Have the flashbacks returned?"
JamNJeff:	And that helps?
Drew24:	Yes. We truly have a heart for each other. We pray for one another, and we make it a point to spend time talking about things we've been through and our different areas of weakness. There isn't much we wouldn't do for each other.
TA.Host:	*What are some things to avoid when it comes to overcoming an addiction to pornography?*
Drew24:	If you're struggling with pornography, you can't just not look at the opposite sex. But you have to watch yourself all your life. You will need to ask God for strength flat-out. It means avoiding inappropriate programs on TV. If you have cable movie channels, like HBO or Cinemax, ask your parents to cancel them, or get a blocking program. Don't tempt yourself!
JeffMan:	But you can't always know which programs are "safe" ahead of time!
Drew24:	Actually, it's a good idea to limit how much TV you watch for many reasons. And when you do watch it, don't watch TV alone. It's too tempting to use the channel flicker and jump over to bad channels.

Jer-Jer: What about magazines? They can be a real stumbling block for guys.

Drew24: Yeah, and not just the obvious skin magazines like *Penthouse* and *Hustler.* Some of the mainstream magazines have been problems for me, too. *Sports Illustrated's* annual swimsuit issue shows everything but, and some mail-order catalogs that come in the house, like Victoria's Secret, can get me wanting more. The whole point is to not let those magazines and catalogs get a foothold in your thought life, but that can be very difficult.

TA.Host: ✦ *How big a problem is pornography with high school teens?*

Drew24: It's huge. It's also a problem that's not being addressed enough in our society. It's being swept under the rug. Our culture is becoming more and more sexually oriented. The music industry feeds off of sex. Every industry in our society, it seems, uses sex to sell something or make money. Sex is used more and more on TV, magazines, advertising—everything.

DanBoy: Yeah, but there's a difference between that and outright pornography, isn't there?

Drew24: It's very subtle. I saw the movie *Jack* not long ago, and in that flick, the ten-year-old boy's favorite thing to do was to read *Penthouse* magazine. That was the cool thing to do. Pornography is seen as a normal stage of development in our teens. When a kid hits ten years old, he should be looking at *Penthouse,*

	or at least that's how the thinking goes. But the damaging effects are becoming better known, and First Amendment defenders are having a tougher time justifying it.
86er:	What's the best way to not get started on porn?
Drew24:	Educating young people about the dangers of porn would be a great start. We've got to tell teenagers why it's wrong and why it's more powerful than alcohol. You can take a drink and not get addicted the first time, but porn is like starting a wildfire—it's pretty hard to put out. If your parents are letting you watch R-rated movies, they'd better be previewing them and talking to you about them too, or you'll be heading down the wrong road.
TA.Host:	*When did you watch your first R-rated movie?*
Drew24:	Believe it or not, it was when I was in elementary school. I watched R-rated movies on HBO and Cinemax with my parents.
TA.Host:	*You were in elementary school and they saw nothing wrong with that?*
Drew24:	No.
TTI:	Did you ever kind of wonder what was happening on the screen?
Drew24:	I have to admit that I didn't know everything that was going on, but it sure made me want to learn more.
TA.Host:	*Have you ever talked to kids about pornography as part of Teen Advisors?*

Drew24:	Not yet. Looking at porn is something many teens don't want to admit to. But maybe this will help jump-start the subject. I tell you, it's needed.
TA.Host:	*Do you see pornography on college campuses as being a problem?*
Drew24:	I think it's a big, big problem on college campuses. There's pornography in the dorms, *Playboy* magazines laying around, and easy access to cable TV. Yeah, it's rampant. But porn is easily found in high schools and many homes, as well. Guys use it to masturbate, and for me, that became an addiction.
Jer-Jer:	Whoa, we're talking the M-word here.
Drew24:	There are a ton of guys struggling with masturbation. It's one problem with teenagers today that's not talked about, but I've met more and more Christian guys who are struggling with it. You might find some homes where porn is talked about, but masturbation? No way.
Jer-Jer:	You mean your parents talked to you about masturbation?
Drew24:	I can't remember the time we sat down and talked about it, but I know we did. It was probably brought up in regular conversation. They told me that masturbation was normal and healthy, part of growing up. But that's not what God would have me do. God's Word tells us not to set our minds on the flesh, and masturbation definitely does that.
86er:	So, bottom line: Is masturbation OK?

Drew24: It's my personal conviction that masturbation is wrong because it's not in the purpose that God created our bodies for. Even though it's not sex with another person, it's the same feeling. I want to encourage teens to save themselves.

TA.Host: *Thanks, Drew, for being so honest. Is there anyone else who wants to talk about pornography?*

Jimbo8: I was introduced to pornography when I was twelve years old by a friend. We turned on Cinemax, and we had a natural curiosity at that age. But I knew it wasn't right.

TTI: Did you want to see more?

Jimbo8: Yeah. It became a habit. I read a quote that said, "The chains of a habit are often too strong to be felt, too strong to be broken." That was me.

86er: So it was really addictive.

Jimbo8: It sure was. And watching porn leads to other things. I wanted to do sexual things with girls. That wasn't good.

TA.Host: *When did you turn the corner on your addiction?*

Jimbo8: Six years ago, but I didn't get turned around until I got caught. Two friends and I were watching a dirty movie in a hotel during a church youth retreat. Someone told the youth leader, and the whole story came out. I got in a lot of trouble.

Jer-Jer: How embarrassing!

FFire:	How prevalent do you think porn is?
Jimbo8:	I think that most every kid has seen it. I wish I could go back to a time when I had not experienced this stuff. I can truthfully state that pornography produces lust toward women.
86er:	Did you ask God for help?
Jimbo8:	Sure. Praying every night and reading Scriptures helped. I had to escape from situations that turned me on. But you know what? I'll have to deal with this stuff the rest of my life.
TA.Host:	*What are some things in daily life that cause you to stumble with this problem?*
Jimbo8:	Skimpy clothes that girls wear at school can be a real problem. Even if the clothes are in style, the guys are only thinking about what's underneath those clothes.
Jer-Jer:	I think girls wearing boxer shorts can be a turn-on for a guy because it's underwear.
Jimbo8:	Seeing a girl with tight, revealing clothing is more of a problem in some ways than seeing her naked. It leaves more to the imagination. That causes problems for a lot of guys.
TA.Host:	*What if your little sister says she has a right to wear what she wants? What do you say to her?*
Jimbo8:	I would say this: "Yes, you have the right. But I'm telling you that wearing that top may cause you problems because you're giving off a 'message' that you may not want to be sending."

TA.Host: *Thanks for talking about this, guys. May God continue to purify your minds as you follow Him, step by step, one day at a time. Stay tuned ... we'll be talking about what to do when life gets tough.*

twelve

Let's Chat: What Do You Do When Life Gets Tough?

TA.Host:	*Can you think of a time when you were really in the pits? What was it like?*
Allie98:	Last year my best friend moved away. I cried for days. I still miss her a lot! :-(
MarGee:	My dad has a drinking problem. Some days it's really hard, but I try not to show it.
Jeremy12:	On November 26, 1995, my father passed away. He wasn't in our house or even a nearby hospital, but hundreds of miles away in a strange state, in a strange town, married to a strange woman. And it hurt.
MarGee:	So your parents are divorced?
Jeremy12:	Yeah. That was tough, too. While I have many good memories, I can't forget the many bad ones, too. Dad was sometimes emotionally abusive. He pushed too hard. His goal in life was to make me into a good softball player, an adequate fisherman, and a strong horseback rider. But no matter what I did, it was never enough. I had to make straight A's, be on the Science Olympic teams, and be associated with the right crowds. All this intense pressure

pushed him over the edge. He was mentally disturbed. My parents divorced in the middle of 1993. I think I handled it well, but maybe I didn't.

KayleneR: A couple of years ago, my grandfather died of cancer only eleven days after he was diagnosed with it. He was so special to me. At that time I questioned many things in my own life, including my relationship with God. It helped me reevaluate my priorities. I want to live each day as if it were my last and to make my life count for something. But there were times right after Papa's death that I was very confused, hurt, and upset.

HeidiLou: How did you deal with it?

KayleneR: My parents encouraged me to show my feelings and my grief. My friends shared their experiences of when people they loved had died. Most of all, they let me know they cared just by listening and being around for me to cry with.

TA.Host: *Has anyone else lost a loved one? Do you have any advice that might help Jeremy or Kaylene?*

OKatie: Get closer to God than you have ever been. Instead of running from Him, tell God your feelings. Let Him minister to you. His grace is sufficient and His strength is perfect.

HeidiLou: When I lost my aunt, I was really mad at God for taking her so soon. But eventually God brought back the peace to my heart. I think you're right about telling God your feelings—

	even the not-so-good ones. That helped me!
Buddyboy:	But my parents broke up a year ago, and I can't see God in any of this.
CynthiaM:	I basically began my life in a broken home. My parents got divorced when I was nine months old! Soon after, my mom remarried, but it wasn't long before she divorced again. Her third husband became a drug addict, so after their divorce, Mom was a three-time loser.
Allie98:	Isn't your mom a Christian?
CynthiaM:	As far as she knew. But she was lonely and searching for love. Rather than going to God, she looked to her husbands. Eventually Mom decided she was tired of living without God, and she became more focused on the Lord. Not long after, she married a fourth time—this time to a Christian man that she'd been friends with for two or three years. Although they have had plenty of hard times, the Lord is victorious. Today, the Lord is first in her life.
MarGee:	Three stepdads! That must have been HARD!
CynthiaM:	It was, sometimes. The only way that I've been peaceful and secure about my life through all this is because I've given Christ my burdens. And that's OK because He knows the plans He has for me ... plans for me to prosper and give me peace.
Jill23Y:	I recently lost my closest friend. I've never hurt so much in my life.
TA.Jen:	Losing a friend is absolutely terrible. When I went off to the University of Alabama, I had only one friend who was going there. His

name was Art, and I must admit I felt relieved that he was also going to Alabama. *Maybe the transition wouldn't be so hard after all,* I thought.

MarGee: Did you like Art? As more than friends?

TA.Jen: No, we were just great friends. He may have had a crush on me. When I became a Christian in seventh grade and started going to church, he befriended me in youth group.

Allie98: So what happened when you got to college?

TA.Jen: I was a little apprehensive, but knew that I had Art to lean on for support. When I arrived on campus, I went through sorority rush. I didn't have much time for him, however, because I got so caught up in making new friends and learning new things. We didn't have much time together during our first semester, but we did have some great late-night conversations, encouraging each other through the first semester.

HeidiLou: Sounds like there's more to the story.

TA.Jen: There is. Christmas came. Art finished his finals two days before me, but he stayed in Tuscaloosa so that we could follow each other home to Georgia. He was worried about me making the three-hour trip on two-lane roads all by myself. But then something happened and we wound up driving separately anyway— and the day after I got home I got a phone call, saying that Art was dead. He had fallen asleep at the wheel. He was within forty miles of home when he ran off the road, flipped his

	car, and broke his neck. He was killed instantly.
Allie98:	Oh no! How TERRIBLE!
MarGee:	I can't imagine how you got through it. You could have been killed, too!
TA.Jen:	It was horrible. I felt really guilty because Art had stayed those extra days for me, and I wasn't there for him in the end. That whole Christmas I dealt with the terrible feeling of things left unsaid and not being a good friend.
Jill23Y:	Why do you think God would allow something like that to happen? I'm still struggling with that question.
TA.Jen:	I don't know. But I have to tell you, I've learned lessons from that, like having relationships right. The idea of not letting the sun go down on your anger took on a whole new meaning for me. In the twinkling of an eye, we can be gone. All of that became so real to me. It taught me *carpe diem*, how important it is to seize the day. And not just what you want to do today, but tell the people around you how you feel about them today.
MarGee:	Didn't you ever tell Art?
TA.Jen:	No. I never told Art the impact he'd had on my life and what he meant to me. It never occurred to me it could end this way. :-(
Jill23Y:	Why is it that we feel so invincible?
TA.Jen:	I think it's because when people our age die, it's not from health-related issues, but rather a sudden tragedy. It seems like we hear about tragic accidents a lot, but until they touch you

they seem unreal. We're told time and time again that we're in the prime of our lives. We should treasure our days. They're going to be gone before we know it. We're not invincible at any age.

Jill23Y: When my friend first died, I didn't cry right away. I just felt cold all the time. Did you experience that?

TA.Jen: One big thing I learned about grief was how I thought I was supposed to be acting and dealing with things wasn't always the way it happened.

KimberlyTT: Did you think you were supposed to be a basket case?

TA.Jen: I didn't know. When I was smiling, I felt guilty that I was smiling. When I was crying, I felt self-conscious. When I wasn't thinking about his death, I thought I should be. It was so overwhelming. It was so different from anything I'd ever dealt with.

MarGee: Did your church friends help you?

TA.Jen: The day after the accident was a Sunday. I can remember walking into Sunday school and thinking, *What am I supposed to say if people ask me if I'm OK? Am I supposed to be strong? Am I supposed to be weak and let them know how I'm feeling?* I thought at the time that it had something to do with it being my first experience with grief. I've learned since then that it doesn't get any easier.

JJohn: Were you angry at God?

TA.Jen: I can remember being angry at God. Just when

Art and I had started having a great relationship and appreciating one another, it was taken away. I was left with all these feelings and no way to deal with them. I knew that I was supposed to trust God and pray for Art's family, but there was a lot of me that needed ministering to as well.

TA.Host:	*Is it different when it's the death of a family member? If so, how?*
TA.Missy:	My youngest sister died recently at the age of twenty-one. Her name was Jenni.
LaToria:	Was it a tragic death?
TA.Missy:	??? It wasn't an accident, if that's what you mean. Jenni had cystic fibrosis, and most cystics don't live past their mid-twenties. Growing up, I never thought I had a sister who was sick. She just had to go to the hospital two or three times a year, to "get a tune-up." Jenni would go in for two weeks, get her lungs cleared out, and life would go on. She led a healthy, normal life, especially in high school, where she was a cheerleader and a model.
MarGee:	A cheerleader! That's incredible!
TA.Missy:	She was special. About a year before she died, though, Jenni started going downhill fast. It was shocking. Jenni got so bad that she couldn't go up the stairs to her bedroom. She was on oxygen the last year of her life.
LaToria:	Do you mind if others talk about Jenni?
TA.Missy:	No, not at all. I love talking with other TAs about Jenni. There were two kids who have

been helped by her story. Just recently I met a girl who's a Teen Advisor. She lost her little brother and I know how she feels. I know what it's like to be in a crowd of people and your heart is broken. You feel like your insides have been ripped out. You feel totally emotionally empty inside, yet you have to put on a happy face.

Annika34: I'm sixteen, and my best friend just died in a car accident. Everyone keeps saying, "It must have been God's will."

TA.Missy: That is one of the most frustrating things about dealing with grief. People will try to give you pat Christian answers.

Annika34: Yeah, like "God is in control."

Jill23Y: Or, "God must have wanted your sister home with him."

TA.Missy: "She's in a better place." When I heard that one, I thought to myself, "But *I'm* not in a better place. I'm still stuck in this world."

MarGee: How did your faith help you through this?

TA.Missy: Remember that parable Jesus told about building your house on the rock, where it will stand? Well, God was laying a foundation in my life in the years before Jenni's death. So when she died, when the storms came, my life didn't fall apart. Jesus was my Rock. I camped out in the Psalms after Jenni died. The Psalms were written by real writers with real feelings and frustrations, talking to a real God.

Annika34: Were you tempted to ask God "why?"

TA.Missy: Not really. Bad things happen to good people

all the time. That's just life. God builds our character through difficulty and trials. It helps us get our priorities straight. Something I learned at Jenni's funeral was people run after things that really, in the long run, are so unimportant. When someone dies, the things that are most important in life all come to light.

MarGee: Like what?

TA.Missy: Well, at Jenni's funeral, I never heard anybody say she drove the coolest car, wore the best clothes, or had the best figure. The things that people remembered and talked about were things like "She was a good friend when I was down" or "She shared Jesus with me." Those are the things I would like to be remembered for.

TA.Host: *Have you ever thought about what would happen to you if you were to die suddenly? If you're not right with God, and want to be, stay with us. If you already know Jesus personally, stay with us anyway—you might be able to help a friend!*

thirteen

Let's Chat: How Can You Get Right With God?

TA.Host:	*To start, let's hear from some of you. What does it mean to you to have a relationship with God?*
Tracey12:	It's the solid foundation on which I build my life, and an umbrella that protects me from life's storms.
SherryV:	It means knowing I'll go to heaven when I die.
HeidiLou:	When life gets too big to handle, it's comforting to know I have a heavenly Father looking out for me.
Caleb42:	Reading my Bible, and living in a way that pleases God.
77Sunset:	I'm not sure I have what you would call a "relationship" with God. How can you have a relationship with someone you can't see or even feel?
Tracey12:	No one—not even the "best" Christian—feels God's presence all the time. Sometimes I have that "ooh-ah" feeling when my relationship with God is great, but other times my feelings tell me that my relationship with God doesn't even exist.
77Sunset:	So why do you keep believing in God?

Tracey12:	Here are three words that I like to think about concerning my relationship with God: FAITH, FACT, and FEELING. These three words are like a train. *Faith* is like the engine, since its power moves the train in the direction it needs to be going. Faith is believing what I cannot see or feel.
77Sunset:	So how do you get faith?
HeidiLou:	It's God's gift to you. You just ask Him for it.
Tracey12:	*Fact* follows *Faith*. The facts of God, which you can read about in the Bible, don't change. God loves me, no matter how I feel. He hates sin. That doesn't change either.
77Sunset:	OK, I'm with you. So what's the third part?
Tracey12:	The last and least important part of the train is *Feelings*. If the whole train followed the caboose, it wouldn't get anywhere. Likewise, our feelings cannot guide us in life. We have to learn that in our relationship with God, our feelings may change, but He never does.
Jenna16:	Feelings can really get you in trouble, if you're not careful. I even dated a guy who wasn't living for the Lord because I thought if it was wrong (and in my heart, I knew it was), then God would let me feel it was wrong. But all I felt was farther and farther away from God.
77Sunset:	What happened?
Jenna16:	After tenth grade, I spent the whole summer genuinely pouring out my heart to Him. I read the Bible to learn more about Him and memorized Scripture to put His words into my mind and heart. That's when I started to realize that

	I didn't have to actually feel Him to know He was there for me. I now love Him so much—more than ever!
77Sunset:	That all sounds great, but I don't think I'm ready for a relationship with God now. Maybe when I'm older. I gotta go … See ya!
HeidiLou:	Careful, Sunset. No one is guaranteed a tomorrow. All we have is today.

TA.Host:	*Why is it important to have a good, strong relationship with God during the high school years?*
Casey048:	There are a lot of struggles high schoolers encounter each day. Without God it's very hard to find the positive answers to our problems.
EErika:	You deal with a lot of rejection in high school—rejection from peers, from teams, and especially when you start dating. Having God as a close friend has really helped me through these times. God still loves me and accepts me like no one else can, or for that matter, ever will.
TA.ML:	My social life in high school was chaotic and uneasy. I'd get in fights with friends. My boyfriends and I would break up. I went through many traumatic experiences because I was such an emotional person. But through it all, God was a real consistent presence for me. I could not have gotten through high school without Him.
TA.Host:	*Anyone out there who hasn't had it so easy walking with God?*

TrentT8: I still don't, sometimes. On the surface, I appear to be Joe Christian. I have been a believer since I was seven. But I've doubted and failed to trust in Christ many times. I've hung in there, because having a relationship with God, makes a huge difference in the way you behave and succeed in the classroom. Knowing God during my low times has given me an extra burst of courage, strength, and perseverance.

Casey048: There have been times when I've strayed from God, just like everyone else. But God is the one person I never have to worry about talking to. No matter what I've done, He still loves me. He is truly my best friend. Without Him, my high school life would be very, very rough! :^)

TravisMan: What are some things I can be doing to make sure I have a close relationship with God?

TaylorG: Get in a Bible study with some good, spiritually solid friends. There's a lot of freedom in a Bible study to ask questions, and this is where you can mature as a Christian.

TA.Anne: It's also important to have someone who is spiritually mature lead the Bible study—like a youth pastor or someone older than the group. They will know how to read the Bible, how to pray, and how to answer your questions. They will be there for you.

TA.ML: I bought a clothbound, blank book and wrote in it every day. I'd start with "Dear God," and then I would tell Him about my day or what I was feeling inside.

TravisMan: Like a journal? How long have you been doing it?

TA.ML: Since my sophomore year. Writing in my journal was such a good thing for me. I'd write down things I could pray about. For instance, I'd write about a boy I wanted to go out with. It was like a diary. I still have it today, and sometimes I'll bring it out and read what I wrote years ago. It's fun to look back and see where God has answered prayers.

Rusty2000: If you're wondering how to develop your own relationship with God, you need to step back and take some time to evaluate your life. Ask yourself: Who am I? What is important to me? What do I really believe?

TaylorG: Just being a TA helps me stay close to God. At my school, being a TA is considered going against the flow. I feel that I am standing up for God by being a TA. Also, I give up lots of school activities and goofing-off time with my friends so I can go on church trips. I think that's a great way to glorify God.

TrishA!: My relationship with God has been one big roller coaster. That's because I hang out with people who don't have the same morals as me. I need to be with Teen Advisors, and I know that. If you don't have a Teen Advisor group in your high school, then hang out with friends who have the same moral standards as you.

TA.Host:	*Any suggestions on keeping the "roller coaster ride" more level?*
PaulM6:	One thing that has helped me has been accountability groups. Right now, I'm involved with a close group of guys.
Everguard:	Tell me more about this accountability group.
PaulM6:	I first heard about it on a youth retreat at church. It's a group of three to five guys. We have a list of questions to ask each other when we meet. After answering the questions, we're able to talk openly about things. We know each others' weaknesses. We can call each other on the carpet.
Everguard:	How often do you meet?
PaulM6:	We meet once a week at our church, usually before school. The meetings take about thirty minutes.
Buckman14:	I have to jump in here and tell you that every time I walked into a room of people, I felt like I didn't belong. I even dreaded going to Bible study because it was such an effort to win approval of everyone there. If I thought one person didn't like me, it ruined my whole day. I was so tired of finding acceptance by working hard. I wanted people to like me and befriend me without any conditions.
MarGee:	Everyone wants that, Buckman.
Jer-Jer:	Yeah, but there's only one place to find that kind of acceptance and unconditional love ... you know what I mean?
Buckman14:	I know. Jesus Christ. He accepts me—faults and all—and loves me the same. My mom

	always says that. She reminds me all the time that my worth comes from God.
TA.Jen:	Your mom is one smart lady.
Buckman14:	One Scripture verse that has really helped me keep my priorities straight is Galatians 1:10: "Am I now trying to win the approval of men, or of God? Or am I trying to please men? If I were still trying to please men, I would not be a servant of Christ."
Angelina16:	Like Buckman, I've often felt that I didn't measure up. I ran cross-country, but I didn't feel good enough until I was number one. I tried out for plays, but I didn't feel comfortable until I got a part. Then once I got a part, I had to be the star getting the standing ovation.
MarGee:	Yeah, once you start looking for approval, it's hard to stop.
Angelina16:	Finally I did, though. I just stopped. Since then, I've kept my eyes on Christ. I haven't had to try so hard, but it's not like all my problems have gone away. I still don't have a boyfriend. I'm not guaranteed any parts in plays. I'm not running cross-county anymore. But I feel better about myself. What a relief that God doesn't love me for what I do or could be. Instead, I know a God who knows my name and my future.
TA.Host:	*Great discussion! It is my prayer that you will continue to grow strong in the Lord, and follow Him always. Stay with us ... we're going to talk*

> *about another very important relationship in*
> *our lives. That's right! Your parents! Stay*
> *tuned.*

fourteen

Let's Chat: All About Parents

TA.Host:	*Some teens think parents are the ultimate all-time drags. For others, their parents are their best friends. For most, it's somewhere in between. What do you think? Talk to me now.*
GinaGina:	My mom is pretty cool. She pretty much lets me do my own thing. She has to ... she works a lot!
Caleb42:	I'm homeschooled, so I see a lot of my mom. I don't mind, though. She teaches me a lot.
SweetBilly:	I wish I could talk to my dad. All he does is yell. And hit me when I mess up. Which is a lot. :-(
HeidiLou:	My mom doesn't hit me ... but I never know when she's going to be happy or mad. It's hard to live with.
Lindsey04:	I think we need to give parents a break. Believe it or not, they want the best for you, even though it doesn't seem like it at times. Your parents love you more than you can imagine, and they would never do anything just to hurt you. I know mine wouldn't!
Gina@12:	Yes, but it seems like my parents live in a totally different world than me.

Lindsey04:	Yeah. Parent World. >8-0 They will worry about you and love you every second of the day. The most important things to remember about parents is that they love us, they were once our age, and they want both our respect—and our friendship.
Cheyenne12:	I lost both my parents in a car wreck when I was eight. It makes me mad when I see my friends disrespecting their folks.... If I had mine, you'd better believe I'd do anything they said!
BranDee:	How sad! Who takes care of you?
Cheyenne12:	My grandmother. I love her, but I sure miss my mom and dad. It scares me, cuz I have to keep looking at pictures to remember what they looked like!
Lindsey04:	Thanks for sharing, Cheyenne. I sometimes forget how lucky I am to have my parents. :-) We need to appreciate, love, and respect parents more. I guarantee that if you look hard enough at your parents, you will not only see yourself in them, but you will also see your best friends.
45678YY:	What can you tell me about getting along with parents?
TomTunes:	I'm amazed at the number of teens who don't think their parents understand what they're going through.
Gina@12:	My parents can't relate to me. They're not the same age, so how could I expect them to?
TomTunes:	The reality is that our parents—and I know this is really hard to believe—were once our age.

They've been down many of the same roads we're traveling now. On top of that, our moms and dads know us better than anybody else—even better than our close friends. They know what's best for us. There's certainly no one who loves us more.

Courtney123: Really? It seems like my dad's busy, and he comes home late from work. He never spends time with me.

ShaRonda: I can relate. When I was younger, my dad had a job out-of-state, and he was gone for nine months. So I was without a dad for nine months. That was terrible on the family, and thankfully he quit and came home, but he was unemployed for a while. That was difficult for us, but we were happy because we had time together.

Rusty2000: Parents aren't perfect. Sometimes they don't see the needs of their children. It's OK to tell them that you need them. Plan something to do with your dad, or better, plan it for him. Make it easy on dear ol' Dad.

Triple888: I don't get along with my parents. What if I can't talk to them?

TA.ML: A lot of people can't. Maybe there are teachers at school you can talk to. If you're involved in a church group, you can talk to your youth pastor or the older kids in the youth group who you feel are making good decisions.

TA.Host: *Anyone here grow up in a home with non-Christian parents?*

LadyErin:	I can touch on that. I come from an entirely different background than a lot of TA kids. My parents aren't Christians. They drink, smoke, and always have wild parties. When I became a TA and showed no interest in that stuff, my parents thought that I was missing out on a good part of life.
SweetBilly:	I'll say! My family isn't perfect, but I don't know if I'd like your situation very much.
LadyErin:	Yeah, you could say my relationship with my parents is a little strange. :0(
RRDonner:	What did they say to you about drinking and sex? Go ahead and do it—just be safe?
LadyErin:	For me, it was more a matter of what they *didn't* say. Other kids had parents who extended their curfews because they were Teen Advisors, but my parents were really out of touch and had no idea what TA was all about.
Gina@12:	Didn't you tell them?
LadyErin:	Sometimes in TA we would write letters to our parents, which can be easier than talking to them directly. One time, I wrote this: *I know that you may not see things the same way I do. And I know that I'm only fourteen and you're thirty-five, but I really think that you should know that this is what I believe and think.*
SweetBilly:	Huh. Betcha didn't give it to them.
LadyErin:	Yes, I did. I would sneak into their bedroom and leave these letters on their bed so they'd find them when they went to bed. I could never confront them verbally.

RRDonner: Did they say anything to you? You must have been nervous!

LadyErin: I was completely intimidated. But it was like I never dropped those letters on their bed. I mean, the next day I'd see them, and they wouldn't say anything. I even looked under the bed to see if my letters somehow fell off. I recently found a lot of those letters in my mother's bedside table. To this day, they have never brought them up.

TA.Host: *Erin, wasn't your situation unusual, not getting any support from home?*

LadyErin: Yeah, it was a bit unusual. I wouldn't say that I was the only one that was like that, however. You'll find that with the increasing number of families breaking up and all the divorce going on, it occurs more. But God has used this experience, and now I am able to reach out to those people who are in the same boat, because they are often embarrassed about it.

HeidiLou: I know what you mean about the "deep freeze." When I started going to church it was the same way with my parents. They didn't try to stop me—but they didn't want to talk about it, either. I decided that I should keep going, anyway. In the end, God is the one I will have to answer to.

RandiDoll: I have a couple of friends who are caught in the middle between their parents, who are divorced. What should they do?

Misty46: That happens to my friend Brandi. Her dad

lives in the city next to the one we live in. He used child support payments as a bargaining chip. If he got what he wanted, he sent the money. It made it really hard on Brandi and her mom.

RandiDoll: What did Brandi do? Did she try to talk to him?

Misty46: No. When they would get together, he'd act like everything was OK, but everything wasn't OK for her. She had a real hard time relating to him. She only saw him a couple of times when she was in high school.

RandiDoll: She must have been mad at her dad!

Misty46: She would tell me about her problems with her dad, but I had a hard time understanding cuz my parents are still married. I felt bad for her. I used to complain about my dad, the little stuff he did. But I felt guilty when I realized that Brandi desperately wanted a good relationship with her dad, wanted her dad to love and care for her. She had a bad situation, and I had no right to complain about my relationship with my parents.

Triple888: What happens if your parents are the ones making the bad decisions?

CharleneJ: My dad is an alcoholic. Seeing firsthand what alcohol can do to a family has persuaded me not to drink. When he's been drinking my dad breaks all his promises, acts obnoxiously, and even scares me. Once he even moved out. He doesn't even realize that I need him and want him in my life.

TA.Host:	*Have you tried to get help for your dad?*
CharleneJ:	I cannot help him or change him. I know deep down that he will never change because he does not want to. He's been drinking for almost thirty years—why should he stop now? I've pleaded with him, tried to explain how he was hurting me—I even sent him an ultimatum saying that if he didn't try harder, I would cut off all communication with him. None of this worked.
Triple888:	Maybe someone else will get through to him ...
CharleneJ:	His girlfriends are all alcoholics, so there's no help on that end. I just don't know what to do anymore. I'm so afraid he will die and rob me of precious time with him. I even have nightmares about him dying because he was drinking and driving.
TA.Jen:	Charlene, it's important that you find someone, an adult you can trust, to confide in about these things! If your mom can't help you, find someone else—a pastor, a teacher, someone! God loves you, and won't leave you alone. But you have to reach out!
45678YY:	Sometimes things get so bad for me at home I think of leaving. Has anyone here tried to run away?
Tony23:	I did once. It lasted one day, until I realized that I was responsible for providing for myself. I was never as lonely and scared as I was that night.
Triple888:	Really! What did you do?
Tony23:	I went to a friend's home. She was a TA, and her parents let me spend the night. She and her

	stepmother talked me into calling my parents. But I was afraid. I had cursed them and all they had done for me and thrown it in their face. I expected them to yell at me and tell me to take a hike—which I had done.
SweetBilly:	My dad would have!
Triple888:	You never know what parents are going to do. They can surprise you sometimes. What did your parents do, Tony?
Tony23:	I was shocked. The first thing they asked was if I was OK. Then they asked if I would meet with them the following day to discuss my coming home.
Gina@12:	What's to discuss? They had to take you back!
Tony23:	I wasn't so sure ... I had acted so bad that they should never have spoken to me again. But when we saw each other, they pleaded with me to come home. Their actions defy all reason. They did everything in their power to get me to return to them. I never realized they loved me like that before.
HeidiLou:	What a great story! :-) Makes me think of the Prodigal Son story.
RRDonner:	Yeah, or like Paul says, "Love never fails" (1 Corinthians 13:8).
TA.Host:	*Do any of you have experience dealing with step-parents?*
EricMan:	I have a stepmom who makes things hard. She tries to be my mother. I don't see her that way.
Robbie15:	She's not going to be your mother, but you are going to have to get along. Try to find some

CynthiaM: I've had three stepdads—and one was even a drug addict! But my mom's present husband is a Christian. I don't always agree with him. But when I remember all the hard times my mom and I had before, I'm thankful he's there for her. And for me.

45678YY: Let's talk about something else. My parents always have to know where I'm going, whom I'm going to be with, and what I'm going to do. What should I do?

TyroneM: That sounds like my parents to a T. They expected to know where I was all the time. If I was going to someone's house, I had to leave the phone numbers, and if I missed curfew by more than five minutes, watch out!

45678YY: Did you ever miss curfew?

TyroneM: Yeah. Once I was with some friends, and I lived about a half hour from my friends. It was a Saturday night, and all of us were supposed to be home at midnight. But in order for me to make it home on time, I had to leave at 11:30 since I lived outside the city.

Gina@12: :-{ That's early!

TyroneM: That night I decided that 12:30 was OK. That way, I could stay with my friends almost thirty minutes more.

HarryHead: Were they up when you arrived at 12:30?

TyroneM: Yup. :^(My dad was waiting. He told me I was going to be punished for disobeying. The next morning they said for the next couple of months, my curfew would be thirty minutes earlier. So now I had to be home on Saturday nights at 11:30.

HeidiLou: When I've been late, my parents aren't nearly as steamed if I just call to tell them where I am and why I can't make it in time.

TyroneM: Yeah. I'm definitely going to do that next time. My dad even said he probably wouldn't have minded if I was late if I had called and asked if I could stay out thirty minutes longer. "But because you took it upon yourself to do what you wanted to do, I can't trust you," he said. "You'll have to earn the trust back. Respect and trust have to be earned. I'm not going to just give them to you." So I earned it—I was in by 11:30 every time!

Gina@12: Man! They really treated you like a baby. My parents don't care what time I come in.

MichaelV: My dad would make a joke about it. "Well, YOU can stay out as late as you want. But the CAR has to be in the driveway at midnight." Since I'm the only one of my friends who drives, he figures he's safe!

TyroneM: My parents weren't treating me like a baby ... they had every right to expect me to call. I just wasn't using my head. But I really learned from that experience. The next year, when I was a senior, I had earned their respect and trust back, so my dad gave me the freedom to make my own curfew. As long as they knew where I was and when I was coming home, I was on my own. That raised my respect

	level for them big time.
JoyT:	I don't think my parents would ever let me set my own curfew.
TyroneM:	I was probably the only one out of my group of friends who could do that. My parents figured I'd be on my own the next year, anyway, so it was a good transition to being on my own!
MeghanM:	My parents told me they'd never expect anything of me that they didn't expect of themselves. They were a strong example of not using alcohol or drugs, of being on time, and they expected the same of me.
TA.Host:	*The teenage years can be rough on both parents and their kids. For many teens, the first time they are truly on their own and making their own choices is when they start going to college. Stay tuned, and we'll talk about some of the challenges TAs and their friends faced when making the BIG MOVE!*

fifteen

Let's Chat: What About College?

TA.Host:	*Let's talk about college. Who wants to start?*
Mallory12:	I'm a junior, and the thought of going to college seems so … strange. Well, maybe not strange. I actually feel kind of afraid about it.
Alaina17:	The prospect of college terrified me! I knew that I wanted to go away to school, but I didn't want to leave high school and my home because I thought the pressures of college would be overwhelming.
BANDIT16:	Not to me! I can't wait to go! Eat what I want, sleep when I want, go to class when I want…. Life will be HUGE!
TA.Jen:	Yeah, but just remember. If you don't study, you won't pass. And if you don't pass, you'll wind up back home! College is NOTHING like high school. It's much more self-directed.
Alaina17:	I think the key to being happy in college and avoiding the pressure of drugs and alcohol is to find true friends.
Mallory12:	But how do you make friends in a new place?
Alaina17:	I had a hard time at first, because in high school I had always lived in the same town, so I never

had to think about making friends. I just had them. My freshman year in college my roommates and I sat in the dorm all day and complained how we didn't have any friends. Then we realized the answer was getting outside our room and meeting people. We had to take the initiative!

HeatherBee: For me, life got better when I went to college and found classmates who are still some of my best friends.

Crystal88: Why is that?

HeatherBee: Because I was freed up to choose my friends a little more. In high school, I was going to a youth group where I felt like I was the only one living for God. In college, I had more choices for friends. I could choose where I went to church and what kind of ministry I wanted to be involved in. On my campus, there were several Christian organizations I could plug into. I could choose to be in a sorority or not.

TA.Jen: I pledged a sorority when I was in college and had a really good experience. Did you?

HeatherBee: It was one of the most nerve-racking things, dealing with a lot of superficial acceptance or rejection. During rush, I walked in and met a dozen girls in five minutes, and they judged me on how cute I was and whether I would be a good fit in the sorority. I visited seventeen houses and met 150 girls in each house in one day. They decided whether to ask me back the next day based on my three-minute presentation.

Gina@12:	So you decided not to pledge?
HeatherBee:	Right. I thought it was more important to be myself. In the past when I've built friendships on superficial things, it's never worked out. At college I became very good friends with a girl who's Jewish. She's very committed to her religion, and she knows that I'm equally committed to my Christianity. While we know we aren't going to agree on our faith, we could still mutually respect each other. That's what being a good friend is all about.
MacyMer:	So is there life after high school? I need some encouragement. College seems so ... grown-up.
Robbie15:	For me, college is a hundred times better than I had ever thought it would be. I was a Teen Advisor for three years in high school, but high school life was still very hard for me. The peer pressure, always worrying what people thought, trying to sort it all out ... I wish I could go back and do it all over again now that I'm nearing the end of my college years. College has just totally changed my perspective, and I feel so much more free to really be myself.
HeidiLou:	College was 100 percent better than high school. I didn't have to deal with the cliques anymore. In college you meet all kinds of people, and really get involved!
AndyN20:	How does Teen Advisors prepare you for college?
MaryKate:	Because of TA, after graduating from high school, I realized that I was going to be leader.

	I joined a sorority, even went to the college parties, but I still kept my Christian values. It proves this quote I love: "If you want to lead the orchestra, sometimes you have to turn your back on the crowd."
TA.Jen:	That's a great quote!
MaryKate:	Now when I come back as a college leader and talk to those still in high school, I tell them to remember that even as you're leaving for college and everything is changing, one thing has to remain constant—your faith in Christ.
45678YY:	Does your self-confidence improve when you get to college?
TA.ML:	It depends on what you base your self-esteem. When I went off to college and pledged a sorority, I was thrown in with 150 girls who were all cheerleading captains in high school, all on the homecoming court, were always Miss This and Miss That. Suddenly I was on an even keel with everybody else. That may happen to you when you go to college. You may look around and see tons of good-looking girls. You need to be confident with who you are on the inside, and not let everyone judge you on the outside.
TA.Anne:	That's one thing TA really helps you with. Remembering to be true to who you really are, and not try to be someone you're not!
TA.Jen:	You may feel like you have to start getting your hair cut every six weeks, shopping at all the right places, and exercising all the time. But doing those things will warp your self-image

	because you'll get so caught up with portraying yourself well on the outside that you'll neglect what's really important—the inside part of you.
LisaMarie6:	What is dating like in college?
TA.Jen:	Dating was difficult for me. In high school, I ran with a group of friends—half were girls and half were guys. Then I went to college. Even though I didn't get caught up in the drinking aspect, I did get caught up in the dating scene. All my friends had dates for football games and formals. I wanted them too!
Gina@12:	A friend of mine was set up on a blind date for her semi-formal. Like a prom in high school.
Courtney123:	You have to be careful with setups, though. You can wind up with someone who looks at life VERY differently.
TA.Jen:	That's true. My freshman year of college, I was set up with a guy. University of Alabama football games are huge social occasions, and having a date for the game was a big deal. Well, this really cute guy asked me out for my first football date, but the day after he called, he found out I didn't drink. So he called me and said, "I don't think I want to go out. I don't think you'll be very much fun."
45678YY:	What a loser!
Gina@12:	Totally classless.
TA.Jen:	I was devastated. If ever there has been a time when I questioned what I believed in, this was it. At home I was known as a good Christian girl who didn't drink and wanted to remain pure. People respected me for that. But in this

large state school environment, nobody even cared that I was trying to stand for things that would make me a godly woman or godly wife someday.

KerryMcD: My good friend recently said, "My boyfriend knows the cutest guy. Let me set him up with you."

TA.Jen: I must have heard that a hundred times. I had lots of first dates, a few second dates, but not any third or fourth dates because I wouldn't lower my standards. There were several times when I went out with people I had no business dating just because I was lonely.

45678YY: Couldn't you just go to a movie or something? You know, just as friends?

TA.Jen: The college dating scene is hard to get used to. So many guys asked superficial questions. If I attempted to get to know my date on a deeper level, I usually got a verbal brushoff: "I don't really think about that stuff." I think that was one of the reasons that I didn't have a lot of third and fourth dates.

KerryMcD: I bet those college boys tried to get you to take a drink, even after you told them you didn't drink. I've heard that guys will use alcohol to lower the defenses of their dates so they can have sex with them.

TA.Jen: I had tons of guys always trying to convince me to drink. I never quite figured that out. But you could be right. They could have been thinking about trying to get me into bed later.

TA.Host:	*For those of you who have been to college, how did you choose the one that was right for you?*
DavidE:	Everyone in my family has gone to the same place. I'm not sure I would choose it otherwise, but since my parents are paying I guess I'll be going there.
HeidiLou:	Some magazines like *Campus Life* list a lot of Christian school ads, and many of them tell you what courses of study are offered. If you know what you want to do, it's a lot easier.
MichaelV:	This year I'm a senior, so I've been asking my older friends what they did about it. The answer's always the same: God will show you.
TA.Host:	*That advice applies to a lot of situations in life. As you learn more about God, through His Word and through others who know Him, He will help you to make better and better choices. Give your future into His hands, then do your homework to scope out the best possible choices. God will always lead you the way that is best. Trust Him!*

sixteen

Let's Chat: How Teen Advisors Changed My Life

TA.Host:	*OK, for this final chapter, I'm looking for postings on how Teen Advisors has been for you folks. Anyone want to take a shot at it?*
BethANee:	When I was a freshman, I was so insecure. I would do anything to make myself not stand out. Well, if you could see me now, you wouldn't think I'm the same person. I'm just about the most outgoing person, and I love attention—sometimes too much! I love to be in front of a crowd.
RachelS14:	How did this happen?
BethANee:	Being a Teen Advisor forced me to be a leader and to speak out. With each year, I'm given more and more responsibility in Teen Advisors, and my self-confidence is soaring.
Darin345:	I think the thing that makes Teen Advisors so powerful is that it gives teenagers a safe environment to address things that really hit their lives.
FreeWill:	Like what?
Darin345:	Lots of stuff. Like, I grew up in a home where Mom drank beer like water, but once I got in TA, a lot of healing took place. I think many

teenagers feel that they're not worthy of a whole lot, and when they feel that way, they don't have anybody to share with. Teen Advisors is a place where they can come and be heard—and loved.

MeghanM: I have been a Teen Advisor for three years now, and I have loved every minute of it. But there was a time one summer, I began to experiment with alcohol to see what was so wonderful about it. I broke my contract, and my closest friends confronted me. I denied drinking and went on with my life. I thought it was none of their business, that it was my life, and I could do whatever I pleased.

Gina@12: That's right. It is your life.

MeghanM: Yes, but as time passed, I began to feel an emptiness in my heart. I loved the people in Teen Advisors and I loved my friends, but I had let them down. I had decided that drinking was not for me!

Courtney123: I've been through so much in my sixteen years on this earth. Divorce, abuse, alcoholic parents, anorexia, severe depression, suicide attempts, low self-esteem, and much more. Before, all I could focus on was the horrible things in my life. Now, they rarely cross my mind because TA has helped me put my life back together.

JoshOOa: Before I became a Teen Advisor, I didn't go to church or read the Bible. I didn't know about God and His love. I was confused and lost. Then I got into Teen Advisors, and their example helped me to trust and love God. They helped me without my even knowing it. If I weren't a TA, I could be a messed-up kid on drugs or alcohol. I'm sure of it because my sister got caught up in drugs and alcohol in high school. I feel that if she had had a TA program in high school, she might not have gotten into that stuff.

MarinET: With Teen Advisors, I know these are the people who will hold me up throughout the year. I want them there when I have a bad time, and I'll be there for them, too.

TA.Host: *What do you mean by people holding you up?*

MarinET: It means doing whatever it takes to help a person feel loved and accepted for who they are. It means making yourself available for people to talk to. Everything that Teen Advisors stands for is about making hard choices when everyone around you is making foolish choices. It's learning to stand on your own two feet and your beliefs.

TA.Host: *What has being in Teen Advisors taught you about other teens?*

LaurenS: If kids could just experience TA, they'd want the intimate relationships we have. It won't happen at school.

TobyMan: There are these two guys I know. One I'll call "Ted"; the other is a guy named "Carter." Ted is a guy who has it all. He has loving, wealthy parents who provide everything he could possibly need: fancy car, nice clothes, and complete freedom. He has tons of friends and plenty of dates. I used to think he had to be the happiest guy alive. But Ted still wasn't happy. He started smoking and drinking, figuring that would fill the void. Then he turned to drugs in his quest for happiness. But none of that has made him content.

TyroneM: Except for the drugs and drinking, it sounds like he has it pretty good!

TobyMan: You'd think so, wouldn't you. Now Carter has little in material possessions. He's got few friends, no dad, and he is physically disabled. People make fun of him behind his back and really give him a hard time. I used to think, *Man, I'm glad I'm not him.* I was wrong. Carter has something Ted doesn't: happiness. Carter found out a long time ago that you can't worry about what you don't have. Instead, you have to content with what you do have. Carter enjoys life and has been a great friend. The lessons Carter has taught me are ones that I'll remember for life. I met Carter through TA.

Drew24: Well, I can tell you what Teen Advisors has taught me. Every teenager at some point struggles with his or her self-image, and in many cases, does things they normally would not do just to gain acceptance. For a long time I was so unsure of myself that I would be afraid to speak to someone, just because I worried if they would like me or not. But Teen Advisors got me through that. The friends I made at the

	Bible study, the retreats, and the tune-ups are some of my best friends now. I realized that these were people who didn't care about how much money I had, what kind of car I drove, or my physical appearance. They cared about who I was, and what my personality was like.
Gina@12:	So you're saying TA keeps you from being stupid.
Drew24:	I guess so. All too often, teenagers will resort to destructive behavior because they think it's the only way to be accepted. Teen Advisors give a much more positive message. Unconditional acceptance is at the heart of the Teen Advisor organization.
LadyErin:	TA made a big difference in my life. At my first TA retreat, each of us was given a "blessing bag." It is a little white lunch bag with your name on it, and you hang it on the walls of the big retreat gathering room. All weekend long, we would write these little encouraging notes to each other on three-by-five cards and drop them in that person's bag. I still read those cards—they've helped me through lots of tough situations. Teen Advisors has blessed me in unbelievable ways, and I hope this book has done the same thing for you!
TA.Host:	*Are you interested in learning more about Teen Advisors? The next chapter will give you more information about how to contact them. God bless you!*

seventeen

Want to Learn More About Teen Advisors?

The video picture on my TV screen was a bit grainy, but I could make out a couple of guys and a redheaded young woman sitting in a large living room. A big Christmas tree, trimmed with bright ornaments and ringed with blinking lights, stood in a corner.

From the bits and pieces I heard, it became clear that this trio knew each other well and had just gotten back into town after their first semester in college. *Home for Christmas,* I thought. *How nice.*

But as the three nineteen-year-olds started talking, I sat up and listened. They were describing why something called "Teen Advisors" meant so much to them.

I heard phrases like "Teen Advisors helped keep me from drinking in my dorm" and "I can stand up to peer pressure at my college since I became a TA." What struck me was that these kids felt good about not drinking, doing drugs, or messing around with the opposite sex. They weren't embarrassed at all.

The video had been handed to me by a colleague at Focus on the Family, where I was the editor of *Focus on the Family* magazine from 1986 to 1997. The coworker, Rick Beggs, had just spent some time in Columbus, Georgia, where he met an incredible group of teenagers. "They've got some teen-to-teen program going on that really seems to be working," Rick said, as he dropped the video in my hands. "These kids don't drink or do drugs. In fact, they sign contracts saying they won't do that stuff!"

After seeing the video, I had to go to Georgia to see Teen Advisors for myself. I called Richard and Dee Dee Stephens, who started Teen Advisors and whose living room had been the site of the filming. I expressed my interest in learning more about the teen group for a possible magazine article in *Focus on the Family* magazine. We worked it out so I would fly to Columbus from my hometown in Colorado Springs, Colorado, during a mid-year retreat.

For three days, I immersed myself in Teen Advisors. I heard several of them speak at a Sunday school class. *Wise and mature beyond their years,* I thought. Then I watched them have fun Sunday afternoon at the Stephens', playing character-building games and even doing a "team climb" over a fifteen-foot wooden wall erected in the Stephens' front yard.

On Monday, I sat in several classrooms while the Teen Advisors did "panels" on drinking and sex for middle school kids at Pacelli High. On Monday evening, I enjoyed "Parents Night," in which the teens and their parents discussed some heartfelt issues.

When I came back to Colorado Springs, I knew I had a story—a story I wanted to share with the several million readers of *Focus on the Family* magazine. I'm reprinting it here so you will have a good overview of what Teen Advisors is all about:

Charting a Different Course

One afternoon after school, a sophomore lad slipped into Christi Ham's classroom.

Visibly distraught, the boy stood near the door. Mrs. Ham, a religion teacher at Pacelli (pronounced Puh-CHELL-ee) High in Columbus, asked the student to sit down and compose himself.

"I can't stand it," he said in a choked voice, as the teacher patted his shoulder. "I can't fight the pressure anymore."

Gently, Mrs. Ham asked what was bothering him. Was he having trouble with his girlfriend? Was it the pressure to party and drink?

"No," the boy replied. "It's all the pressure *not* to drink."

In a flash, Mrs. Ham understood. Because of a peer counseling group on campus called Teen Advisors, drinking was no longer cool at Pacelli. The sophomore, who liked to down beer at weekend parties, was tired of hearing his classmates tell him to abstain from alcohol.

The Pacelli Teen Advisors—and similar groups around the country—have turned peer pressure into a positive force. The message not to drink or do drugs is coming from the students themselves—not parents and school officials, a concept that makes the Teen Advisors so interesting.

The Columbus program began in 1987 when Richard and Dee Dee Stephens' eldest daughter, Mary Lawson (that's her first and middle name), was attending Pacelli, a Catholic high school with more than half of its students coming from Protestant denominations.

Back then, every weekend was marked by bitter arguments between daughter and parents. Why? Mary Lawson wasn't allowed to go out to parties. A popular cheerleader, she yearned to be accepted by the "in crowd," but that crowd usually huddled around a beer keg every Friday and Saturday night.

As Christian parents, Richard and Dee Dee wanted to do something proactive about the peer pressure. They were convinced that if several high school students would take a stand against drinking, drugs, and premarital sex, more would follow. In addition, they were sure impressionable freshmen and junior high students would readily listen to upperclassmen.

That spring, Dee Dee and another mother, Kit Newlin, asked the principal of a Columbus-area junior high if they and several students could talk to an eighth-grade class about dating. The moms were joined by four Pacelli High students, including Mary Lawson (who had come around to her parents' point of view) and Kit's daughter, Missy. They answered questions the eighth-graders had written anonymously on three-by-five cards.

The first panel was so well received that Dee Dee telephoned eight more students and asked if they would be interested in talking to junior-highers about drinking.

Dee Dee mentioned one little catch, however: The teens had to agree not to drink for the rest of the school year. "I asked another junior whom I knew was drinking to take the pledge," remembers Dee Dee. "I knew if she would do it, ten kids would follow her. She said yes, and since then, I've found that more kids will take this step if they know their friends are going to stand with them."

Then Dee Dee and Kit accompanied the dozen students to a PRIDE (Parents' Resource Institute for Drug Education) workshop in Atlanta, where they heard about a Teen Advisor program developed by Diane Chenoweth and Syd Schnaars for Olentangy High School, a public school in Delaware,

Ohio. Dee Dee purchased a manual and went to work tailoring a Christian-based program to fit the needs of Pacelli's four hundred students.

"Sitting at the conference, it was like lightning struck," says Dee Dee. "I knew it could work in our area, too. Just before school started, Richard and I put the word out, and forty-two students agreed to attend a weekend retreat to kick off the school year."

At the retreat, the Stephenses organized games and activities that brought the students closer together, much like a summer football camp. "By Saturday night, the kids had really jelled as a team," recalls Dee Dee, "and they wanted to go out and make a difference in their school." On Sunday afternoon, she and Richard presented the teens with contracts stipulating that they would not drink alcohol, take drugs, or use tobacco products for one year.

When Mary Lawson inked her pact, she received a dose of self-confidence to stand against negative peer pressure. "I made a commitment that I knew I had to live up to," she says. "And I did."

Learning More

As Teen Advisors has grown, so has its scope. They meet at least one Sunday afternoon a month at the Stephens' home to talk about how to avoid drinking, dealing with sexual pressure, getting along with parents, and the importance of self-esteem.

But the main purpose of Teen Advisors is their work with the Pacelli freshman class, who have to wait until they are sophomores before they can become a TA. Several times a month the upperclassmen meet with freshman classes by leading small groups that precipitate more intimate discussions.

Want to Learn More About Teen Advisors? / 177

"Our seniors and juniors," says Dee Dee, "are saying to the younger students, 'Hey, we've been there, and we're going to tell you what it's like not to drink and not to get physical with your boyfriend or girlfriend.' When you're a freshman, you will listen to someone two years older, even more so than your parents."

In a way, this arrangement sets up an unexpected system of accountability. How? A Teen Advisor knows the freshmen are watching him closely to see if he backs up his word.

But what happens if a Teen Advisor stumbles and parties hearty? "If you know someone who breaks the contract, you're bound to go to that person and ask him to turn himself in," says a Pacelli senior. "If that doesn't work, you're supposed to turn him in yourself. If you don't, then you've broken your contract."

Teens who have slipped up appear before the Teen Advisor Honor Council, a panel of six elected by other TAs. Notice again that accountability is coming from teen to teen. (Although Teen Advisors espouse abstinence, sexual purity is not part of the contract because the teens didn't feel comfortable discussing the sex lives of their friends.)

"We want those who have broken their contract to be honest. If they are sorry and want to remain with the group, they have to apologize to all the Teen Advisors. They also have to tell their parents—perhaps the toughest part of all. Then they are given a punishment, which is usually a Saturday afternoon of community service."

Another student, Becky Davidson, says signing the contract is a big commitment. "It's not fun and games. Even if there had ever been times when I wanted to break my contract, I wouldn't have because not only had I signed it before other teens, I had signed it before God."

Back to School

It's a Monday morning in Mrs. Rivard's eighth-grade class at St. Anne's, a parochial junior high school. This is the first class of the day for the thirteen- and fourteen-year-old students, who are dressed in their blue-and-yellow school uniforms. Ten Teen Advisors walk in and sit before the students. Mrs. Rivard introduces the group, then adds, "The Teen Advisors are here to talk to you about drinking and to answer the questions you wrote out last week."

The eighth-graders appear excited, but they also take pains to be cool. They don't notice Dee Dee slipping into the back of the classroom, where she monitors all the Teen Advisors' panels.

The TAs are given permission by Pacelli to miss class several times a month to speak before various junior high classes in the Columbus area. Because of the success of the Pacelli program, school authorities recognize that the Teen Advisors reach younger students in ways adults never will.

"Drinking—and the pressure to drink—is one of the top problems facing teenagers today," begins Randi Dean, a senior. "And alcohol is the most widely used drug," chips in cheerleader Kristie Wheeler. "It kills more people than any other drug."

Several other TAs pick up the beat. "The younger you are when you start drinking, the greater the chances you'll become an alcoholic," says Adam Conard. "After an adult starts drinking, it can take five to fifteen years to become an alcoholic. Once a teenager starts drinking, it can take only six to eighteen months to become an alcoholic."

Rusty says everyone on the panel has taken a firm stand against drinking, noting that all the Teen Advisors had signed one-year contracts not to drink alcohol. "When you get to Pacelli," he tells the rapt eighth-graders, "don't plan on drinking beer if you want to be cool. That won't be the way to go. You know those beer commercials with the hard-body guys and Swedish bikini teams? Well, those aren't the usual drinkers. A beer drinker is usually a couch potato with a big beer belly."

The eighth-graders giggle, and then one raises his hand. "Have you ever had anything to drink?" he asks.

Nearly everyone on the panel nods yes. Most say they tried beer or hard liquor at a friend's party while they were in junior high. One girl says her mom offered her sips of Bacardi rum while the family was vacationing in Florida. "Imagine," she exclaimed, "having pressure to drink from your parents!"

Dee Dee leans over to a visitor. "Four years ago, when the Teen Advisors heard this question, they usually answered, 'I was getting drunk last year, but now I'm not.' Now, it's 'I had a beer back in junior high.' That's how I have seen the pendulum swing in just five years."

Talking About Sex

The last time the Teen Advisors did a "sex panel," they received a cool reception at a Columbus public school eighth-grade class.

The eighth-graders may have listened to the Teen Advisors' pro-abstinence message, but they weren't buying it. When the TAs talked about the consequences of an unplanned pregnancy, one eighth-grader raised her hand and described her seventeen-year-old sister's pregnancy and safe delivery of a little boy. The father married the sister, she said, and they were doing just fine.

It was a "take-that" statement hurled at the panel. Jennifer Young remembers being taken aback for a moment, but after a quick, silent prayer, she plunged ahead. "I am really happy that it worked out for your sister," she said, "but she's an exception. She's maybe the one out of a hundred that works out, but for the other ninety-nine, their lives are ruined." She also told the eighth-graders it's OK not to do it, that she's a virgin, and she is going to save herself until marriage.

The Teen Advisors continued that "wait-until-marriage" theme at another sex panel before a seventh-grade class at St. Anne's. "We want to tell y'all that safe sex is sex with the person you marry," began Shawn Scott, a senior.

The Teen Advisors then shared statistics about the low effectiveness rate of condoms and the danger of AIDS and other sexually transmitted diseases. "And there's no condom that protects your heart, your mind, and your self-esteem," said Lauren Jones. "When you start having sex, pretty soon that's all you'll have in common. You can't go back to kissing because sex is progressive."

The panel then entertained questions from the seventh-graders:

"How far should you go on the first date?" Their answer: Although it's expected to kiss on the first date, you certainly don't have to, the panel agreed. Anne Stephens, a junior and one of Dee Dee's three daughters, said she went with a guy for four months before they kissed. "That made it a lot more special."

"When should I start dating?" You should talk it over with your parents, the panelists replied. Group dates are the best because that won't put you in a compromising position.

"Should I go out with a guy even if I don't like him?" Shawn

took this one. "Guys don't want 'pity dates,'" he said. "You'll both end up having a lousy time."

The strapping, six-foot, 180-pound Shawn then turned the discussion to premarital sex. "I'm eighteen, and I'm a virgin, so don't let people out there tell you no one's a virgin anymore," he said. The seventh-graders didn't make a sound as they hung on his words. "I think being a virgin makes me more of a man. It takes more character and more willpower not to have sex these days."

The Generations Meet

An important part of Teen Advisors is the once-a-quarter Parents' Night. With eighty parents seated in the Pacelli auditorium, Dee Dee began the evening by describing the world in which today's high school students are growing up: 10 percent of teens are alcoholics; two out of every ten unmarried teen girls become pregnant (and half of them abort); date rape is a common problem on college campuses; and teens are committing suicide in higher numbers than ever before.

Then Dee Dee told the parents that she asked the TAs at a previous meeting to write a paragraph—anonymously—to their parents. They were to pretend that this would be their last communication with their parents.

Dee Dee read several to the attentive parents, some complimentary, some poignant:

There are so many things I have to tell you. I am so sorry for all the pain I have caused you. I was mean, selfish, and hateful. I'm not proud of that. I thought I was always right; I have told you I hated you often. But if I were a parent, I would do things just the way you have done them.

I know I'm not the easiest person in the world to get along with. But it always seems that you somehow accept me for who I am. I really respect you for not giving up on me. I love you and pray to God that I will carry the morals and values you have taught me.

I've always loved you, yet you have treated me like an outsider. I wish you could include me, trust me, and be my friend. I'm not as horrible as you think I am. I wish I could be given a chance.

Happy Days

As Parents' Night came to a close, several fathers spoke up about Teen Advisors. "When my boys went to Pacelli fifteen years ago," said Joe Wheeler, "it was, 'Who can spin the most doughnuts in the parking lot and drink the most beer?' My oldest son was the class president, and it took him fifteen years to get off chewing tobacco. He started chewing when he was on the football team because it was the macho thing to do in those days. He didn't quit until the birth of his first child.

"You should see this school now," continued Joe. "It's as calm as can be, like back in the fifties. Fifteen years ago, if a boy stood up and said he was a virgin, they would have laughed him out of the school.

"What I like is that Kristie, my sophomore daughter, is getting a good education. She doesn't have to worry about all this drinking and drugs stuff. Yup, this school has really turned around."

We included the Teen Advisors' address at the bottom of the article, and it wasn't long before their mailbox was jammed. The organization is still receiving letters more than five years after the article appeared, and in all, they've responded to over two thousand letters from every state in the union and from more than a dozen countries. Parents are writing and asking how they can start a Teen Advisors group in their hometown.

If you don't have Teen Advisors in your high school, TA would love to help you! We offer several resources, including videos, retreat planners, and network information that may be valuable to you and your parents. For more information, including current prices, please contact Teen Advisors at the number listed below.

Getting in Gear: Everything You Need to Know About Teen Advisors
This is really everything you need to know about Teen Advisors. Several new chapters meet the needs of those starting a new program (dealing with obstacles, how to adapts the program, etc.). Also included are many proven Teen Advisor programs including Parent Night, a Mini-Retreat, and a freshmen lock-in.

Shifting Gears: Teen Advisor Classroom Sessions
Everything you need to present classroom sessions to younger teens. All sessions are outlined, all activities explained, and all handouts included. This resource includes material for the following ten sessions: Charting Your Course (Introduction to TA/Peer Pressure), All Stressed Out!, Getting Along with Parents, Making and Keeping Friends, The Gateway Drugs (Alcohol, Marijuana and Tobacco), The Cold Within

(Prejudice), Why Wait (Abstinence), True Value Isn't Just Hardware (Self-Esteem), The Monster Within (Eating Disorders), and Why Date?

Also available: Shifting Gears video series: Six individual classroom sessions are available on video, which show the Columbus Teen Advisors presenting the sessions as written in the resource. These are an excellent companion to the *Shifting Gears* resource:

> Charting Your Course (50 mins)
> All Stressed Out! (45 mins)
> Getting Along with Parents (45 mins)
> The Gateway Drugs: Alcohol, Marijuana and Tobacco (45 mins)
> Why Wait? (40 mins)
> Self-Worth: Seeing Your True Value (40 mins)

Teen Advisor Retreats
These retreat programs are unlike anything on the market. Each retreat planner contains over 100 pages of games, talks, small group activities, and schedules. There are three retreat programs available, each of which is a complete minute-by-minute description of the weekend. Retreats could be used in their entirety or specific sessions lifted and adapted for your own use.

> Retreats:
> This is War: TA Retreat Number 1
> Run the Race: TA Retreat Number 2
> Feed and Seed: TA Retreat Number 3

Ripple in the Water Video
Produced in 1994, this video provides an excellent description

of the program as well as scenes from classroom sessions, retreats and assorted TA activities.

National Teen Advisor Network
Want up-to-date information about Teen Advisors? Join our network to receive our newsletter as well as announcements of new ideas, resources, but also gives you "technical" support whenever you need it.

Other Services
Day Long Workshop: What is Teen Advisors? This is an excellent program for those areas desiring to start a program. Teen Advisors will run a 6 hour workshop for adults and teenagers outlining the program and giving at least two classroom sessions of your choice. Expenses plus fee.

Here's how to contact Teen Advisors:

Teen Advisors
P.O. Box 6468
Columbus, GA 31917
e-mail: teenadv@mindspring.com

Teen Advisors has a web site that is under construction at the time this book is printed. You'll be able to find them on the Internet at www.teenadvisors.org